Tales of the Bachelor Mine

The story of the Bachelor Mine and Syracuse Tunnel
on Ouray County's Gold Hill

JANE BENNETT

Foreword by Duane Smith

San Juan Publishing

Second Edition
Printed in the United States
10 9 8 7 6 5 4 3 2 1

Library of Congress Control Number: 2005930825
ISBN: 0-9771376-0-0

San Juan Publishing
PO Box 1055, Ouray, Colorado, 81427
www.sanjuanpublishing.com

Cover photo: miners of the Bachelor Mine, *Denver Public Library, Western History Collection, X-61106.*

Back cover: 1886 map of the Red Mountain Mining Region, *San Juan County Historical Society;* Miners inside a mine building in Ouray County, Colorado, *Denver Public Library, Western History Collection, X-61113;* Louis Duke, blacksmith, Bachelor/Syracuse Mine Tour, *Craig Henry.*

Book and cover design by Kathryn Retzler

Dedicated to Doris Gregory.

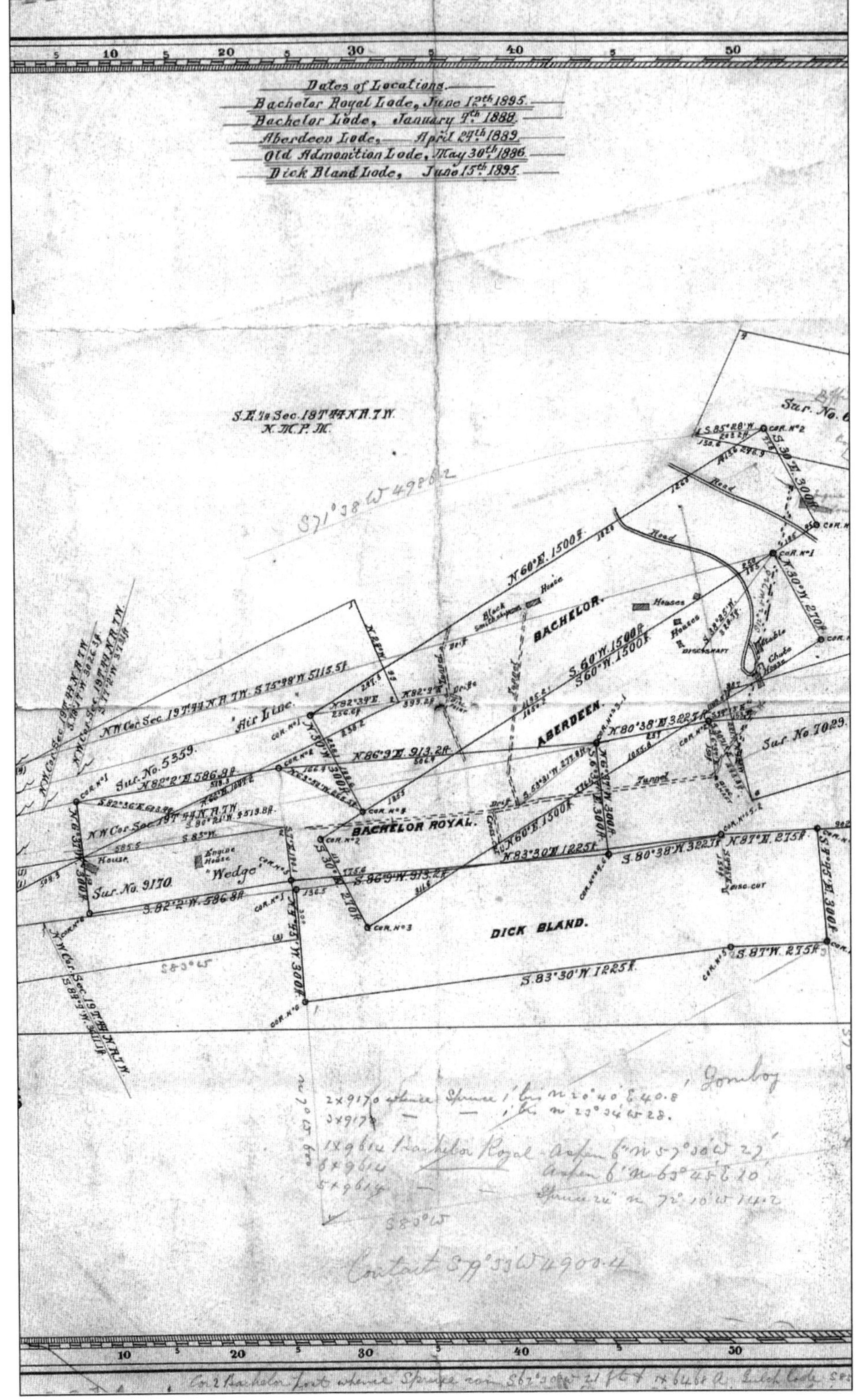
Dates of Locations.
Bachelor Royal Lode, June 12th 1895.
Bachelor Lode, January 7th 1888.
Aberdeen Lode, April 24th 1888.
Old Admonition Lode, May 30th 1886.
Dick Bland Lode, June 15th 1895.
S.E. ¼ Sec. 18 T 44 N R 7 W.
N.M.P.M.
Sur. No. 6
Sur. No. 7029.
Sur. No. 5359.
Sur. No. 9170.
BACHELOR.
ABERDEEN.
BACHELOR ROYAL.
DICK BLAND.
"Air Line."
"Wedge"
Engine House
House
Road
Road
Houses
Houses
DISC. SHAFT
Chute House
Tunnel
Contact

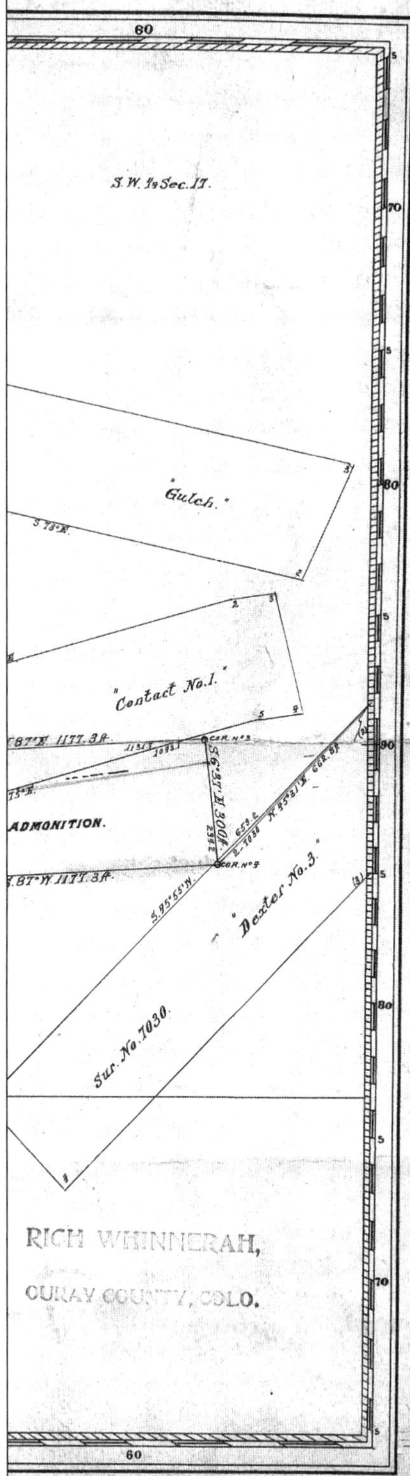

Claim Located ____________________________ 18

Mineral Survey Nº ____________ 9614

LOT Nº ____________

Montrose, ____________________ Land District.

PLAT

OF THE CLAIM OF

GEO. R. HURLBURT ET AL,

KNOWN AS THE

BACHELOR ROYAL, BACHELOR, ABERDEEN, OLD ADMONITIO AND DICK BLAND LODES,

IN ____UNCOMPAHGRE____________ MINING DISTRICT,
____OURAY____ COUNTY, COLORADO
Containing an Area of ____________ 39.45 ____ Acres.
Scale of ____300____ Feet to the inch.
Variation 13°35' East
SURVEYED ____________ July 12th 1895 BY

F. L. Biddlecom, ____________ U.S. Deputy Mineral Surveyor,

The Original Field Notes of the Survey of the Mining Claim of
Geo. R. Hurlburt et al,
known as the
Bachelor Royal, Bachelor, Aberdeen, Old Admonition
and Dick Bland Lodes,

from which this plat has been made under my direction
have been examined and approved, and are on file in this Office,
and I hereby certify that they furnish such an accurate descrip-
tion of said Mining Claim as will, if incorporated into a patent,
serve fully to identify the premises, and that such reference
is made therein to natural objects or permanent monuments
as will perpetuate and fix the locus thereof.
I further certify that Five Hundred Dollars worth of labor has
been expended or improvements made upon said Mining
Claim by claimants ____ or their ____ grantors, and that
said improvements consist of four drifts, two tunnels, two
shafts, a cross-cut, a cut and part of a tunnel, as appears by the affidavit of the deputy surveyor,

that the location of said improvements is correctly shown
upon this plat, and that no portion of said labor or improvements has been included in the estimate of expendi-
tures upon any other claim.
And I further certify that this is a correct plat of said Mining
Claim made in conformity with said original field notes of the
survey thereof, and the same is hereby approved.

U.S. Surveyor General's Office.   Thos. D. Robinson

Denver, Colorado   U.S. Surveyor General for

November 16th, 1895   Colorado

Contents

Acknowledgments

I would like to gratefully acknowledge the help I received from the following people and organizations in writing this book: Larry & Maxine Adams, Herbert Anderson, Sue Babcock, Paul Boyd, James Burke, Jack Clark, Corey Clickner, John Crim, Carl Dismant, Louis Duke, Al Fedel, Doris Gregory, Elwood Gregory, Ginny Harrington, Tom & Linda Hash, Roger Henn, Brian Jacobs, Bill Jones, Bob Larson, Gemma, Irene & Dominic Mattivi, Jr., Cora Kay McCarty, Mary McCready, George & Glenda Moore, Nick & Harry Peck, Duane Smith, William H. Snyder, Barbara Spencer, Francis Stewart, Robert Stouffer, Gerald Swanson, John Trujillo, Roger Young, Jim Wetzel, Dick Zanett, Ouray County Historical Society, Delta County Historical Museum, San Juan County Historical Society, Colorado Historical Society, Western Geneology Department, Denver Public Library, and Ute Indian Museum.

A great many people helped and encouraged me with this project, and I thank you all. My sincere apologies to anyone I've inadvertantly overlooked above.

Foreword

I would have been more or less than human if I had not gone mad like the rest.
Cartloads of solid silver bricks, as large as pigs of lead, were arriving from the mills
every day, and such sights as that gave substance to the wild talk about me.
I succumbed and grew as frenzied as the craziest.

Thus wrote that would be Nevada miner Samuel Clemens, better known today as Mark Twain. He ventured into the Territory during the glory days of silver in the early 1860s.

The same could be said for the first prospectors and miners in the San Juans and for the men who finally brought Ouray's Bachelor Mine into bonanza. A person catches gold or silver fever and it can develop into a life long malaise or can lead to death deep in a mine.

The San Juan Mountains have attracted attention since the days of the Spanish in the 18th century. Hoping to find gold or silver, they entered northward from New Mexico and left behind legends of lost mines and buried treasure. It was not long after the 1859 Pike's Peak gold rush that prospectors ventured into these isolated, ragged, and sky-touching mountains. The abortive rush of 1861 produced no wealth, but the mountains still beckoned and back came the prospectors in 1869.

The 1870s saw the first serious mining as well as permanent settlements in mountain valleys and canyon bottoms. Mining towns and camps took root — Ouray, Silverton, Rico, Animas Forks, Lake City, Howardsville, and others — providing the miners the base they needed to develop their mines.

First it was gold, then silver in the 1880s, and gold again in the 1890s as the international price of silver collapsed. Copper, lead, zinc, coal and later uranium were found in these mineral mountains.

Mining attracted others besides miners to come and make their fortunes. The storekeepers, saloon owners, lawyers (lawsuits followed rich strikes like bears to honey) and a host of folk settled in the communities. In the river valleys north and south, ranchers and farmers arrived who sent their animals and crops to the mountains.

In the 1880s, the railroad reached Silverton and Ouray. Every mining district desired rail connections, the fastest cheapest, most comfortable, and nearly year around (except when hitting a San Juan snow slide) means of transportation available. The really profitable mining days came with the iron horse.

It was in this background that the Bachelor Mine was opened. It operated in one of the United States' great mining districts in the San Juan Mountains. Ouray County, which produced nearly $78 million dollars worth of gold, silver, copper, and zinc from the 1870s through 1923, helped the district gain that distinction.

Duane Smith

Introduction

Gold Hill — what a romantic name. There are many "Gold Hills" sprinkled across the West; almost every mining camp with gold values had one. Some were grand and some were just rocky nubs, but Ouray's Gold Hill is one that lived up to the glamour of its title. "Glamour" is a word that means "a magic spell," and in that sense, it is a word that fits Ouray's Gold Hill.

I first found out about Gold Hill through the Bachelor/Syracuse Mine Tour, about twelve years ago. I was marketing Ouray then, for the Ouray Chamber Resort Association, and the mine tour was one of our major attractions. The tour takes visitors into the Syracuse Tunnel, which is only one of ten levels of the Bachelor Mine. After more than 100 years, the workings of the mines that comprise the Bachelor Group are so extensive that no one living knows just how extensive they really are. Working at the mine tour is a sort of summer camp for adults, and staff members tend to return year after year because it's so much fun. I became one of them.

The familiar Ouray landmarks look different from the vantage of Gold Hill. They seem even more beautiful, if such a thing is possible in such a beautiful place. Up there, life seems full of mysterious possibilities. The veil that separates the present from the past is very thin at the Bachelor/Syracuse: it's the next best thing to a time machine. The old miners always talk about the camaraderie of working in the mines, and that sort of thing still happens among the Bachelor's staff and friends. Some of the best friends I've ever had, I made at the mine — especially the dashing blacksmith, now a tour guide and my other half.

In 1995, some of the Bachelor/Syracuse staff decided to put on a barbeque dinner/show to dramatize the Bachelor's colorful history. Corey Clickner wrote and sang original songs for the show, and Bob Petersen played rhythm guitar, and

The Diggers performing at the Bachelor/Syracuse outdoor cafe, 1995. (That's me on the right, impersonating a Tommyknocker!)

© Mary McCready

Mary McCready was our marketer and all-round "band aide." I did character sketches between songs: the Prospector, the Miner's Wife, the Shady Lady, the Tommyknocker, and so on. Louis Duke demonstrated hand steeling. He drilled into a small boulder as the rhythm section for one of our songs. That made him our "rock" musician. We had a great time, and so did our audiences. We called our show "The Diggers," which is one of the things miners call themselves. Among the places we performed "The Diggers," we were especially proud to be on the bill at Ridgway's jewel-box Sherbino Theater the night of its grand reopening after extensive historic restoration.

Tom and Linda Hash, who ran the Bachelor/Syracuse tour business at the time, asked me to write in book form the stories that we dramatized. They were convinced the Bachelor had many other fascinating tales to tell, and they were right.

Six years of interviews and research went into the writing of this book. During that time, Ouray has lost all but a very few of its miners. I was fortunate to have had the opportunity to talk to mining gentlemen like John Crim and Al Fedel while they were still with us. I've learned to appreciate what a very special type of courage it takes to work in a hard rock mine, and as I've learned more about the mines on Gold Hill and the lives that were lived there, my affection for them and for the old mountain has continued to grow. For me, it truly is an enchanted place.

Tale One – The Men
The Lucky Ones

In a blinding snowstorm, George Hurlburt slogged into the mining camp of Ouray.[1] It was only a speck in the swirling clouds of snow — a handful of raw, new buildings that sprang up just the year before, in 1876. That's when prospectors from the south found gold and silver in a beautiful but remote box canyon in the rugged San Juan Mountains of south-western Colorado. Hurlburt's trek through the storm from the Los Pinos Indian Agency was hard work, and dangerous, but he was no greenhorn.

A boxer, a teetotaler, an athletic man in his prime, Hurlburt had already spent strenuous years as a frontier surveyor defining properties that made other men rich. Someday it would be his turn, and Ouray was his destiny.

Hurlburt was born in Silver Lake, Indiana, in 1847. His parents moved to Kansas, and by the time Hurlburt was 21 years old he'd learned surveying, helping to lay out the streets of Wichita.[2]

George Hurlburt as a young man, circa 1892
Ouray County Historical Society Collection

Chief Ouray and his wife, Chipeta

Ute Indian Museum, Montrose

Once again his parents moved, this time to the Territory of Colorado, and Hurlburt went with them. 1873 found him surveying around Walsenberg, and then Silverton. In 1877 and '78 he decided to do something different, and tried his hand as an Indian trader. Hurlburt's skill as an interpreter led to a position as a clerk at the Los Pinos Ute Indian Agency. It's not certain what his duties there were, since the term "clerk" can mean many things.

He liked the Utes, and had many occasions to talk with the famous Chief Ouray. He described Ouray as "a very dignified person, sedate, usually very quiet and spoke but little, using a sort of mongrel Spanish, totally devoid of grammatical order."[3] Ouray and his wife Chipeta were always welcome, and the only Indians who ever sat at the table with the Agent and employees of the agency, Hurlburt said.

While at the Los Pinos Agency, Hurlburt became friends with the Agent's brother: fellow surveyor Charles Wheeler. After leaving the Agency, Hurlburt and Wheeler surveyed many of the San Juans' mining claims and town sites. Hurlburt helped to lay out the towns of Telluride and Ridgway, and tried placer mining on the San Miguel River along with Charles and two of the other five Wheeler brothers. During the winter of 1879-80, Hurlburt carried mail between avalanche-ridden Ames and Rico. In 1883 he started a formal surveying partnership with Charles Wheeler and settled permanently in Ouray.

Many times, the two had to survey right through the San Juans' brutal winters. Hurlburt was usually found working alongside his crew, enduring the same hardships they did. Once he was hurled 2,000 feet down a mountainside near Silverton by an avalanche. Miraculously, he was able to dig himself out and was extremely lucky to have survived. He later became known for helping to rescue many other avalanche victims.

For more than ten years, Hurlburt and Wheeler were driving forces in the development of the San Juans. Through the last half of the 1880s and into the '90s, their ad in Ouray's *Solid Muldoon* newspaper advertised "Wheeler & Hurlburt, Civil & Mining Engineers. All work in the Surveying Line attended to with accuracy & rapidity. References: Any responsible citizen of Ouray or adjoining Counties." When Charles

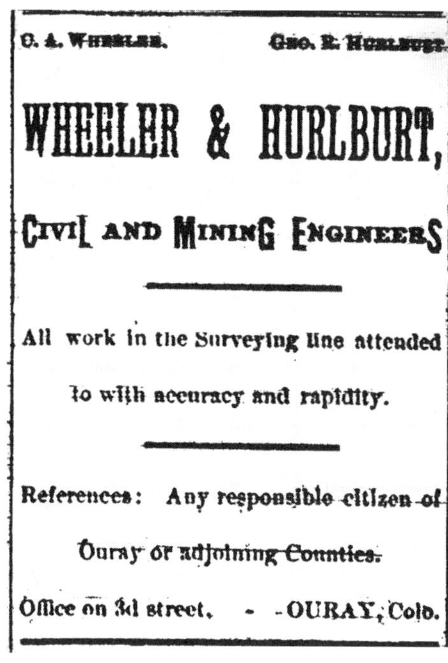

Hurlburt & Wheeler Surveyors ad that appeared in the *Solid Muldoon* throughout the last half of the 1880s and into the 1890s

Wheeler died suddenly of pneumonia, Hurlburt continued his partnership — but with Charles' nephew, Walter Wheeler.

One promising area that needed surveying was the aptly named Red Canyon, north of Ouray. The Dexter and the James V. Dexter were two of the earliest mines there, and Red Canyon Creek later became known as Dexter Creek. Hurlburt surveyed several mines on the creek, including the El Mahdi. He enjoyed talking to the El Mahdi's affable chief cook, Charley Armstrong, and lived at the El Mahdi boardinghouse whenever he was working in the area. One can imagine the two seasoned adventurers standing in the boardinghouse door, looking thoughtfully out toward what they believed was the probable direction of the El Mahdi's vein of ore.

Like George Hurlburt, Armstrong had also taken a degree from the San Juans' school of extremely hard knocks. Just a year or so earlier, in 1883, he had been chief cook at the Virginius Mine in the Sneffels mining district when a massive avalanche took out the boardinghouse and most of the other buildings at the mine.

Miners pose near the shafthouse of the avalanche-prone Virginius Mine on Mount Sneffels. Circa 1910. Charley Armstrong was buried by an avalanche at the Virginius.

Denver Public Library, Western History Collection, X-62115

Armstrong, who was standing near the dining room wall when the snow slide struck, was flattened against the wall and completely buried in snow, but not injured. Fighting for air, he was able to push his arms upward until they broke through the snow.

After regaining his breath, Armstrong inched his way along the wall toward the root cellar door. By the time he got there, he had already been in the snow for ten hours. Dumping the vegetables onto the floor, the shivering man wrapped himself as best he could in potato sacks, and waited. He was in the root cellar another twelve hours before he heard the sounds of a rescue party. He yelled, but it was no use. Groping around, he finally found something to hammer with and made the rescue party hear him at last.

Emerging from the root cellar, Armstrong found the avalanche had killed four fellow miners. As he started trudging for Ouray, he passed the rescue party starting out with a grizzly cargo of corpses lashed on sleds. Less than half a mile down the mountain another slide hit the rescue party, taking the dead men and most of the party of thirty down the mountainside. Luckily, none of the rescuers were killed, but two of the dead men were buried so deeply it was two years before their bodies were recovered.[4]

Armstrong reached Ouray before he heard of the second snow slide. His arrival caused quite a shock, since his friends had just read in the paper that he was one of those killed at the Virginius. The next year found Armstrong working at the El Mahdi in an area that, compared to the Virginius, was conspicuously free from snow slides.

Few others agreed with Armstrong and Hurlburt about where the El Mahdi's vein was headed. Nevertheless Charley Armstrong, his younger brother Alf Armstrong, and a man named J.T. Brown filed a claim in 1888 and called it the Bachelor.[5] It may be, as local tradition has said, that all three were bachelors at the time. However, "Bachelor" was a fairly popular name for a mine. There was

A miner leads a mule train down an icy, snow-covered trail toward a mill in Ouray County, Colorado.

Denver Public Library, Western History Collection, Walker Art Studio, X-61994

another Bachelor claim south of Ouray in the Red Mountain Mining District, for example. There was yet another Bachelor near Creede, in the east central San Juans, and that one grew to have a whole town named after it. As we will see, marketing was everything in the early days of the mining boom. A catchy name drew investors. Perhaps "bachelor" was a word that could be counted on to appeal to a large number of overwhelmingly male mine investors.

Whether he was a bachelor or not, about a year later Brown sold his interest to Hurlburt. The Armstrong brothers and Hurlburt could only afford to work the claim in spurts as their finances allowed, however. County records show Charley Armstrong signing over his interest in the claim time and time again to secure loans and borrow money — most often from Judge Theron Stevens — but he always redeemed his pledge. After some years the three exhausted partners had

Jesse Frank Sanders

only managed to drive about 500 grueling feet into the mountainside.

What they needed, they decided, was an investor. It's not known how they found J. Frank Sanders, but find him they did. It was a happy day for all of them.

Jesse Frank Sanders was born in Broome County, New York, the youngest of four sons. At seventeen he left home and went to Pennsylvania, where he learned blacksmithing and became a machinist. He worked at his trades for a number of years in Pennsylvania, and on February 23, 1879 he married Catherine Ferguson.[6]

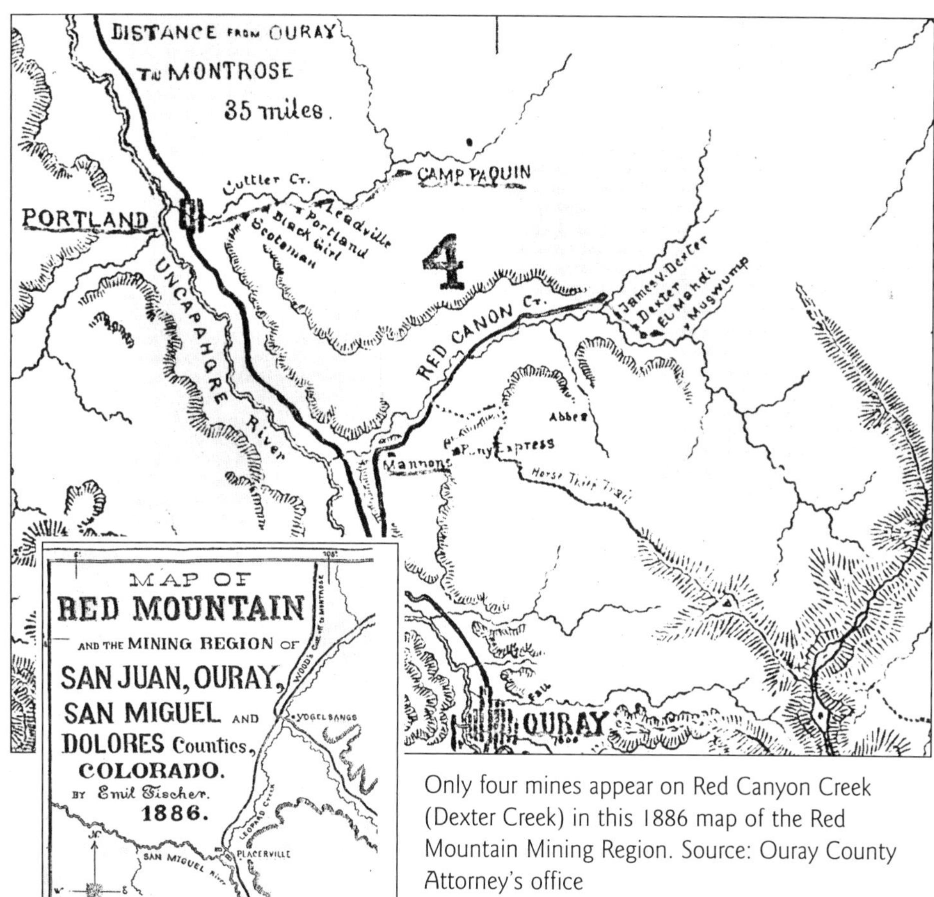

Only four mines appear on Red Canyon Creek (Dexter Creek) in this 1886 map of the Red Mountain Mining Region. Source: Ouray County Attorney's office

San Juan County Historical Society

Catherine's father had tried his hand in Colorado during its earlier years, but soon returned to Pennsylvania. Perhaps his tales of adventure and opportunity made J. Frank want to seek his fortune there too, for in 1880 he bid farewell to his young wife of only a year and emigrated to Alma, Colorado. There he alternated between working at his trades and prospecting. By 1887 Ouray had became his base of operations. It's likely that his interest in prospecting and mining was what brought him together with Charley Armstrong and George Hurlburt.

The three are said to have been a lively bunch. They loved a good time and they loved to bet on things, anything — even which raindrop would make it to the bottom of a windowpane first. The Bachelor must have appealed to Sanders' sporting nature, for in November of 1894, he bought Alf Armstrong's interest in the mine for the princely sum of $2,000. Since the going price for a one-third interest in a mining claim was about $100 at the time, it seems Sanders already knew that he was betting on a sure thing.

The fact that Sanders had $2,000 to risk (about $40,000 in today's money) implies he'd had a fair amount of success up to that point. Sanders' father had joined him from Pennsylvania a couple of years earlier, though.[7] Did the father sell property back home before joining his son in Colorado? Did the money Sanders put on the Bachelor represent the family nest egg? Was it every cent they had? What did J. Frank's wife back in Pennsylvania think of her husband's adventuring? If only we knew. Luckily for all of them, Frank's bet paid off.

One morning not long after, when the dust and smoke from the night shift's dynamite charges cleared, the miners discovered they'd pierced a large body of silver ore. Soon, ore worth from $250 to $400 a ton was being hauled down Red Canyon Creek from the Bachelor.[8] The three had struck it rich. It's a testament to the richness of the mine that even after the disastrous Silver Crash of 1893, when the price of silver fell twenty-five percent in four days and many other silver mines went belly up, all three partners are said to have realized about a quarter of a million dollars each from the Bachelor in just a few months' time.

By 1895 the Bachelor was the highest-producing mine in the Ouray area, in spite of the economic depression caused by the Silver Crash. According to the Delta newspaper, the monthly net income of each partner in that year averaged between $10,000 and $12,000, while in March it shot up to $27,000.[9] After that, the Bachelor was customarily referred to in print as the "famous" Bachelor Mine. For the next hundred years, it proved to be one of the strongest producers in the Uncompahgre Mining District and one of the most reliable mines around Ouray.

The two miners on the right each hold a singlejack hammer, which can be wielded with one hand while holding the steel drill with the other hand. Source: Rosenstock '56.

Denver Public Library, Western History Collection, X-61105

Three miners in the Pony Express Mine, later a part of the Bachelor Group. Working by candlelight, two of the men use a hand steel and a doublejack to drive a blasting hole. One man hits the steel with the large doublejack hammer while the other turns the steel a quarter turn after each blow. The fellow on the ladder holds a pick. Circa 1890.

Denver Public Library, Western History Collection, X-61081

Cora Hickman Hurlburt, circa 1895

Ouray County Historical Society Collection

The stalwart Bachelor was even one of very few mines that stayed open during the much longer Depression of the 1930s.

George Hurlburt did not remain a bachelor for long. Within a year after the mine came in, he married pretty and capable Cora Chambers Hickman in Las Animas, Colorado. They set up housekeeping in a small cabin at the corner of Fifth Avenue and Fourth Street in Ouray, but soon enlarged it into a graceful and spacious Queen Anne home. It remains one of the most attractive Victorian homes in Ouray. In 1895 Cora gave birth to the couple's first child, a daughter, Helen, who later became the district judge for Ouray at a time when there were very few female attorneys, and virtually no female judges. The example and encouragement of her two pioneering parents undoubtedly left their imprint on Helen.

Hurlburt used his wealth to benefit almost every member of his extended family. According to granddaughter Cora Kay McCarty, he set them all up with a farm or a business while he was in the money. George and Cora were well-liked, and pillars of Ouray society. In 1904, the Hurlburts welcomed their second child, a son, George Junior.

For all his obvious intelligence and professional expertise, it was Cora who had the head for business while George was naive, according to granddaughter

McCarty. Perhaps that explains Hurlburt's unfortunate investments in the Bank of Ouray and the Grizzly Bear Mine. The mine turned out to be disappointing, and in 1907, when the bank went under and closed its doors, Hurlburt found his fortune rapidly ebbing way. Undiscouraged, Hurlburt returned to his profession of surveying, "which he did with as good grace and happy spirits as if he had never made a fortune."[10]

By age 11, George Jr. was helping his father in the field. For almost ten years they continued to survey in the San Juans and also in the Grand Junction area. The Hurlburts bought a ranch in Horsethief Canyon west of Fruita, and used it as a winter home. Hurlburt sold his interest in the declining Bachelor to Charley Armstrong, and left Ouray with Cora to live at Horsethief Canyon year-round. Great-nephew Bill Snyder later recalled that the Hurlburts' place there had a small dance floor, and was a very poplar spot for parties.

In 1924, however, the Hurlburts had returned to Ouray and George was running for County Surveyor, a post he is said to have inaugurated as Ouray County's first County Surveyor.

George Hurlburt, circa 1924, about the time he ran for Ouray County Surveyor

Courtesy Cora Kay (Hurlburt) McCarty

His campaign literature didn't mention that, but it did assure voters that, "When surveying is to be done, no job is too hard or hazardous for him, as shown by his recent horseback trip alone to the Empire Chief Mine near Lake City, and his work in surveying the Bostwick Park reservoir sites, which won comment in the *Montrose Press*; and numerous other plucky achievements."[11]   Not bad for a man of 77.   A family photo taken about this time shows a distinguished and dashing silver-bearded gentleman on horseback, ramrod straight in the saddle and ready for anything.

Tombstone of George Hurlburt, Cedar Hill Cemetery, Ouray, Colorado

© *Louis Duke*

It was on a Sunday, April 28, 1935, that Hurlburt went to the Cuttigan ranch about a mile and a half south of Ridgway to do some surveying. He wasn't alone, but as evening approached his party separated and Hurlburt started for the road with his transit under one arm and his chain in the other. The rest of the party took another route. When Hurlburt didn't meet them at the highway they became alarmed and called Sheriff Jess Wood. Searching through the night, Sheriff Wood found Hurlburt's body just before daylight. Evidence showed he had slipped on very steep terrain and slid quite some distance down the mountain before his head struck a boulder, fracturing the back of his skull. A professional to the end, he fell with his surveying transit wrapped protectively in his arms. When found, the instrument was still in good working condition. Sadly, the same could not be said for George. The Ouray newspaper remembered him as "a kindly man who held the respect and friendship of all who knew him."[12]

Charley Armstrong lived on until 1940. With the early proceeds of the Bachelor's bonanza, he bought homes for his mother and sisters in Denver.

Armstrong created quite a stir when he chartered a special Pullman car in Denver, taking a private party of mining and business leaders including Dave Moffat, president of the Denver & Rio Grande Railroad, on a well-publicized junket to Yellowstone National Park. Armstrong paid everyone's expenses for the trip.

After the high-grade ore in the Bachelor had been mined there was still plenty of ore of a lower grade, but Sanders and Hurlburt lost interest. As a personal venture, Armstrong bought his partners out and built a mill near the mine to treat the lower grade ore. He also made other investments. Along with Frank Sanders, he invested in the Mascotte Power Company of Delta.[13] Hoping to repeat the Bachelor windfall, Armstrong bought and worked other mining properties in the Ouray area, but none of them compared to the Bachelor. In the early 1920s, Armstrong even spent two summers with a helper trying to find a new body of ore in the Bachelor with the aid of a divining rod, but to no avail.

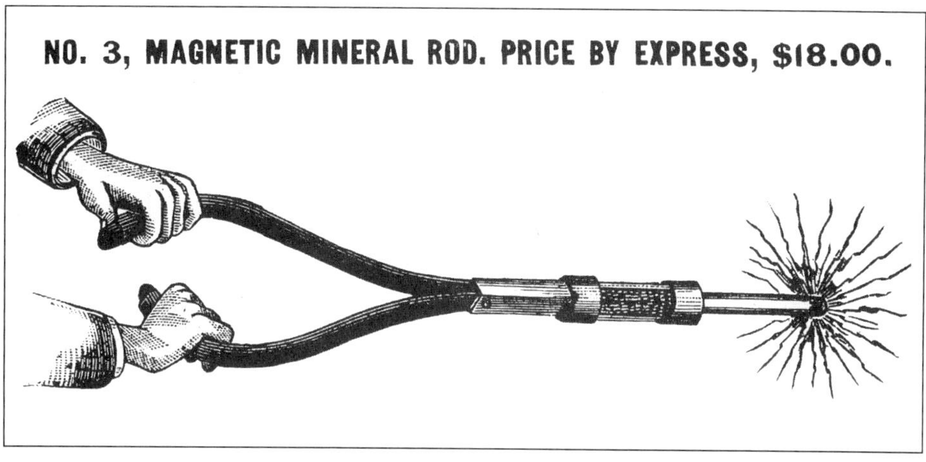

Mail order catalog ad, circa 1890

Ironically, Armstrong did come close to another fortune once. In 1897 another well-known Ouray mining man, Tom Walsh, realized one of his rather lackluster Imogene Basin silver claims had gold in it. Quietly, he began to buy up all the neighboring claims through a third party in order to secure his advantage. Walsh used a third party because he thought if people knew what he was doing the prices would skyrocket. In this he was correct, for the part-owner of the neighboring Oro Cache later declared under oath that "he would have increased the price of the Oro Cache to Mr. Walsh, had he known to whom he was selling it."[14]

Tom Walsh

Ouray County Historical Society Collection

This aggrieved mine owner had a partner — none other than Charley's brother Alf Armstrong. Alf had continued to invest in mines, and also bought and sold quite a bit of real estate in Ouray. On February 1, 1897, Alf gave his brother Charley power of attorney in order to sell his share of the Oro Cache to one S.A. Osborne, and the Oro Cache promptly became part of Walsh's Camp Bird mining group. Although opinions differ, it seems that part of the Camp Bird vein may even extend to the Oro Cache. The Camp Bird mines made Tom Walsh extremely rich, while Alf Armstrong signed away his second chance at a fortune — and once again, his brother Charley helped him do it.

One wonders what kind of relations the two enjoyed toward the end of their lives. Alf died in 1923 at the age of 61, after a career as a miner, painter and paperhanger, and owner of a garage business[15] located on the first floor of the Wright Opera House in Ouray, which he also owned.[16] Today, he lies in an unmarked grave at Cedar Hill Cemetery next to his big brother, Charley.

Charley Armstrong was the only one of the three partners to remain a bachelor. Tall, blonde, and likable, Armstrong was a man's man who also moved easily in society — something not all miners would have or could have done. He arrived in Ouray from Lake City in 1882,[17] and by 1884 his name began to appear in the Ouray newspapers on lists of those attending social events that included mayors and judges, doctors, lawyers and their wives.[18] Local historian Roger Henn, who was born and raised in Ouray, said he remembered Armstrong toward the end of his life as a frightful practical joker, and one of the "Oak Street crowd" of movers and shakers. Julius Sonza, who later came to own the Bachelor, customarily referred to Armstrong as "The Gentleman." [19]

In spite of the reasonable investments Charley made after he struck it rich, over time his money dwindled away. In that, the Great Depression certainly played a large part. By the time he died at the age of 83 much, if not all, his property had been sold for taxes. During the winter of 1939-40, an especially hard winter of record snow and low temperatures, an item in the *Ouray County Herald* announced that "Charles Armstrong is quite ill and unable to leave his apartment."[20] Two months later Armstrong checked into Ouray's Spangler Hospital. Dr. Spangler's

Charles Armstrong's tombstone, Cedar Hill Cemetery, Ouray, Colorado

© Jane Bennett

private six-bed hospital was located on the second floor of the building where the Swiss Store is now, between Fifth and Sixth Avenues on Main Street.[21] Dr. Spangler was the only doctor in town and primarily ran a clinic for employees of the huge Idarado Mine, south of Ouray. Just three days after checking into the hospital, Armstrong died. Charley Armstrong never married, but instead spent his lifetime pursuing Lady Luck through the wild and beautiful San Juan Mountains.

J. Frank Sanders took the money he made from the Bachelor and moved to Delta where he was joined by the patient Catherine, and there the couple raised five children.

J. Frank Sanders family. Standing, in back, J. Frank and daughter, Dora. Seated in front, Catherine, holding Elizabeth, Charles, Cora and Robert on the lap of J. Frank's father, Henry.

Courtesy Larry & Maxine Adams

The J. Frank Sanders home in Delta, Colorado. Circa 1900. The home was torn down in June of 1986 to make way for a parking lot.

Delta Historical Museum

He started a grocery business and soon gained controlling interest in the Farmers and Merchants Bank. It turned out much better for him than Hurlburt's foray into banking did. The Delta paper referred to Sanders as "a handy man with a coin," and so he was. Along with many other business and buildings Sanders initiated, he and a man named Ray Simpson built the Anna Dora Opera House in Delta. The name was a combination of their two daughters' names.

Sanders served two terms as Mayor of Delta and, covering all his bases, was active in the Elks, Odd Fellows, and Masons. He died of a stroke in 1922 at the age of 68. One biographer said of him, "There is scarcely any element of good in the community, industrial, commercial or moral, that has not felt the force of his creative mind and the impulse of his directing hand."[22] A pretty saintly epitaph for an old San Juaner. Hopefully, he also found the time to make a few friendly bets.

Tale Two – The Mountain Gold Hill

The wild San Juan Mountains were born of fire — not just once, but many times. Thousands of catastrophic explosions battered and kneaded the hardest rock, building the mountains up and tearing them down.

Sometimes, with unimaginable force, exploding gases blasted into small fissures, enlarging them and forcing them thousands of feet through solid rock while lining the new walls with material torn from the older parts. In the Ouray area, one large and familiar intrusion of this type came to be known as the Blowout. Rather like a boil, the Blowout swelled and deformed the rock layers all around it, forcing them upward.

Gold Hill

Photo of Blowout today, taken from across the Uncompahgre River looking east.

© Louis Duke

When the Blowout stopped rising, it was still a mile below the surface. The San Juans as they look now were nowhere in sight. The epoch of eruptions that gave them their shape came later.[1]

Besides causing the Blowout, the Earth's explosive forces sent cracks filled with broken material running through the surrounding rocks. This broken material solidified under pressure and chemical influences. The resulting intrusion is called a clastic dike: "clastic" from the Greek, *klastos,* meaning broken, and "dike" because, like a dike, it makes a wall between two things. In this case, it is a wall of foreign material between two parts of the same rock formation.

The Bachelor and American Nettie dikes are found running through the mines for which they are named, but others protrude through the surface all over the San Juans. One that can easily be seen runs parallel with the east side of U.S. Highway 550, just three tenths of a mile south of mile marker 101. In fact, it is best seen looking southeast from mile marker 101. The exposed dike forms a perfectly vertical wall that is especially visible toward sunset, when it throws a long shadow.

Besides the dikes, more cracks also split the dark heart of the mountains as heat-blasted rock started to cool. These fissures slowly filled with hot mineral

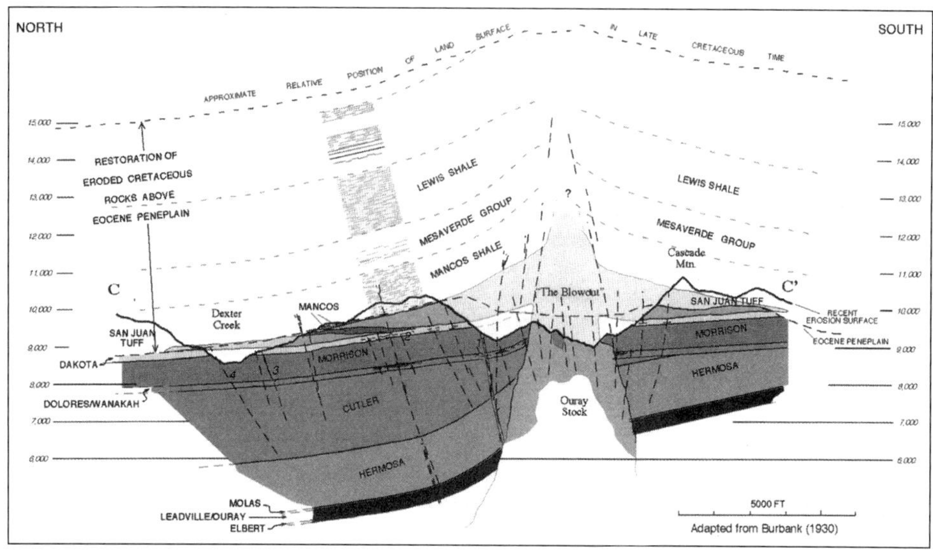

Cross section of the Blowout. Adapted by George Moore (from Burbank, 1930); Colorado Scientific Society. Used with permission.

Ouray County Historical Society Collection

solutions pushed up with enormous pressure from below. The many mineral hot springs around Ouray and Ridgway are all that's left of this ferment. Its force may not be completely spent, however. In 1877 the hot springs both at Ouray and Ridgway all shot ten feet in the air, according to witnesses.[2]

As the hot solutions rose upward through the cracks, they cooled and deposited their minerals. Gold, which can be deposited under moderate pressures at moderate temperatures, was left at the higher, cooler levels. Silver tended to be deposited lower down.[3] The earth-shattering forces that made clastic dikes also made other, more open deformations in the rock that slowly filled with mineral solutions. While some of these became nothing more than fairy-like caves lined with sparkling crystals, others filled with more valuable minerals that were later hurrahed as "rolls" and "bonanzas" by ecstatic miners.

All of this was of very little interest to the first people to travel the San Juans. For thousands of years, the only humans who walked there were the Ute Indians and their ancestors. They prized the mountains for their cool summer temperatures, healing mineral springs, abundant game, and exalted spiritual environment.

One of the best-known and well-established trails used since prehistoric times became known as the Horsethief Trail. Running hundreds of miles from the San

Along the Gold Belt Trail. A miner and two burros loaded with supplies. Circa 1885.
Collection, W. H. Jackson sample album; Colorado Book III; no. 66.
Denver Public Library, Western History Collection, William Henry Jackson, 1843-1942, WHJ-561

Luis Valley across Saguache into the San Juans, it eventually dropped down into the Uncompahgre Valley by way of Dexter Creek.[4] It was a marvelous way for anyone stealing horses from the more easterly tribes to vanish quickly into the mountains. The Horsethief Trail still exists, and remains one of the most popular, if more strenuous hikes in the mountains around Ouray.

In the early 1800s, white fur traders and prospectors followed old trails such as Horsethief into the West. Although there may have been limited mining before, the 1870s saw the first big mining strikes made in the San Juans. Educated mining men, hardened Civil War veterans, and hopeful foreign immigrants all braved the rugged mountains. The first group came because they knew a good prospect when they saw one; others came because they had little or nothing to lose. Furthermore, Western mining booms like the spectacular California Gold Rush of 1849 seemed to show that anyone could get rich over night. In his book *A Guide to Mineral Collecting at Ouray Colorado*, Ervan Kushner paints a vivid picture of what happened next.

> *News of the ore discoveries spread swiftly, as it always does. Literally hundreds of mining claims were soon filed. Eager stock promoters quickly flooded the urbanized areas of the East seeking subscribers for the sale of stock issue of mining companies some of which had not even assayed their claims. There was no Securities Exchange Commission in those days, and it was truly a Caveat Emptor process. Lurid promises of great wealth and quick return of investment were made to an easily receptive and gullible buying public.*
>
> *Even the names of some of these mines conjure up the various types of appeal which were made to the investor: "Wheel of Fortune," "Little Balm of Gilead," "National Belle," "Yankee Girl," "Torpedo Eclipse," "Joker," "Newsboy," "Bright Diamond," and "Coming Plenty." As to the latter, $250,000 was expended in developing the mine and as of the day the mine shut down permanently, not one cent had been returned to the investors.[5]*

Most mining companies never made money for anyone except the suppliers, saloon keepers and prostitutes in town. Today, approximately 10,000 shafts, tunnels and prospect holes within a ten mile radius of Ouray are mute reminders of the mining frenzy that reached its height about 1900. Cascading north over the

Windham Silver Mining and Smelting Company operations near Ouray, Colorado. A mule train makes its way down the hill (on the right). Circa 1885. Source: Samuel Tanenbaum.

Denver Public Library, Western History Collection, X-60848

passes from Silverton, the flood of miners pooled at first in the Mineral Point, Red Mountain, and Canyon Creek areas.

The first discoveries at Ouray were made in 1875. By 1876, the thriving mining camp incorporated as a town, and the prospecting frenzy spread out in all directions. Each winter, when snow choked the trails and avalanches blocked the passes, the prospectors either retreated to town or holed up in the mountains like bears, afraid (or unable) to leave their claims. Each spring, a fresh horde of treasure seekers poured into the San Juans.

The Utes were not pleased with this invasion of their "Shining Mountains." Although they agreed to treaties that were supposed to limit how far the whites could prospect, and though U.S. soldiers were sent to enforce the agreement, the tide of newcomers was unstoppable. Like kerosene on a fire, each new find stoked the flames of prospecting fever and a new wave of intruders would head for the hills. Some of the hills they headed to were the promising ones north of Ouray. By 1877 the Red Canyon, or Dexter Creek mines rated their own section in a mining report published by the *Ouray Times*. "Another Rich Discovery In The Red Canyon District" trumpeted the *Times* in August of that year, announcing the discovery of the Black Silver Mine with "a large body of ore: chlorides, ruby and brittle silver."[6]

Ruby and brittle silver — enchanting words that conjure visions of a glittering treasure cave. Ruby silver is an almost magical sulphide of arsenic

Frame lodging house at Windham (see photo on left; house is on right of picture). Notice the birdcage by the door, small child in front by the baby carriage and woman riding sidesaddle on the far left. Circa 1885. Source: Samuel Tanenbaum.

Denver Public Library, Western History Collection, X-14165

and silver that has a beautiful red color, but the color dulls very quickly once exposed to the air. Not everyone was prone to lose their senses in the search for treasure, however. The town of Ouray was just four years old when R.W. Woodward and S.T. Tyson, "celebrated mining engineers and assayers," wrote the Windham Report of 1880. With it, the Windham Silver Mining and Smelting Company hoped to interest stockholders in building a mill to compliment the smelter they'd built two years earlier on a tract four miles north of Ouray. The conservative and carefully worded report mentions two mines already located in Red Canyon: the Dexter and the Black Silver. The report was optimistic about the future of its own and neighboring holdings, reminding stockholders that:

> *The above list is confined to the mines of the Uncompahgre Mining District, and includes in the main only producing mines. There are also hundreds of prospects which are likely to develop into equally good mines. It should moreover be remembered that the country is not half prospected and that as many more good mines will be found in the next ten years. Thus far only such veins have been located as have prominent outcroppings. Development has hitherto gone forward under manifold difficulties and has necessarily been slow owing to the absence of roads....*
>
> *Development has also been slow because our mines were mainly in the hands of poor men. In 1878 not a single mine in the district was owned by capitalists. Within the past twelve months many mines have been purchased by rich men and strong companies who are able to develop*

Miners near Ouray. Notice boy on the left and the fellow with the snappy straw "boater" and pipe on the right. Circa 1885. Source: Rosenstock '56.

Denver Public Library, Western History Collection, X-61105

Miners pose at the Calliope Silver Mine, Ouray, Colorado, 1884. Source: Rosenstock '56.
Denver Public Library, Western History Collection, G.H.A. Photo, X-61102

their properties. This change of properties will result in rapid development of our best properties and a largely increased output of ore....

When one considers the manifold difficulties which have heretofore attended mining operations in this section, he may well marvel that so many of our mines have been worked at all. It is a high tribute to their excellence that so many of them have been worked and have paid so well.[7]

It's a little difficult to think of all the frenzied mining activity then taking place as representing "slow" development, but the Windham Company did build its mill north of Ouray, conveniently located close to the promising Red Canyon area. In 1883 Ouray's colorful newspaper, *The Solid Muldoon*, reported that "Quite a number of prospectors are scouring the country north of town. Carbonates is what they sigh for."[8]

Carbonates react readily with ore-forming solutions, making them an ideal site for the deposition of ore, and Red Canyon had formations practically made to order.

In 1881 the Calliope Mine north of Red Canyon Creek caused a sensation on what came to be known as Carbonate Hill. It was followed by the Dexter No. 2, El Mahdi, Mugwump, and American Nettie, all south of the creek and all surveyed in 1885 by George Hurlburt. The American Nettie was primarily a gold mine and caused the mountain south of the creek to be called Gold Hill, but that fact wasn't fully appreciated until after the Silver Crash of 1893.

Meanwhile, silver was still king and every year more silver mines cropped up in Red Canyon. The area became known as the Pacquin Mining District, named for pioneer Moses Pacquin who prospected on Cutler Creek with his sons. Their home base appears on an 1886 map by Emil Fischer under the military-sounding name of "Camp Pacquin." On the same map, Lake Lenore shows as "Mannon's Lake." The Mannon ranch was a large and important one, and at least some of the Red Canyon strikes were made on Mannon's land. The Pacquin District is alternately shown as the Uncompahgre District on many maps.

In 1887 Hurlburt surveyed the Pony Express Mine, which turned out to be a strong producer, but by 1890 the Calliope had consolidated into a group of mines including the Dexter Numbers 1, 2, 3 & 4, the Rumpus, the Iowa Chief, the Calliope Numbers 1 & 2, and more, making the Calliope group the biggest thing on Red Canyon Creek. That changed, however, when the American Nettie tapped into very rich gold ore.

Seen from Ouray, Gold Hill is dominated by the enormous Blowout. From afar, the Blowout appears relatively soft, seeming to have burst or melted from the center. It was the focal point of mineralization when ore bodies began to form in the Pacquin District, and several early strikes were made in the Blowout. It has an incongruous rusty yellow or golden color compared with the neighboring cliffs, and that might have helped the mountain to become known as Gold Hill.

Illustration of Bachelor Dike by T.A. Rickard in *Across the San Juan Mountains*, 1907.

Clastic dike as seen from U.S. Highway 550 at mile marker 101.

© Louis Duke

However, most of the values taken out of the mountain were in the form of gold, and that's the primary reason it became known as Gold Hill. The mountain north of Dexter Creek became known as Carbonate Hill, and most of its values were in silver. The Bachelor sat in a transitional zone between the two and had some of both metals, along with others. It's also true that after the 1893 Silver Crash, when the American Nettie was producing serious amounts of gold, it was a godsend for the Ouray economy.

The silver crisis had been coming for ten years or more. Before 1893, U.S. currency was backed by both silver and gold and the government bought 4.5 million ounces of silver a month through the Sherman Silver Purchase Act to make coins.[9] When the Act was repealed in 1893, and the price of silver plummeted, many mines — and even banks — had to close. The resulting depression lasted for years. The American Nettie hit its stride in the early 1890s when Ouray needed it the most, making the name "Gold Hill" a source of pride

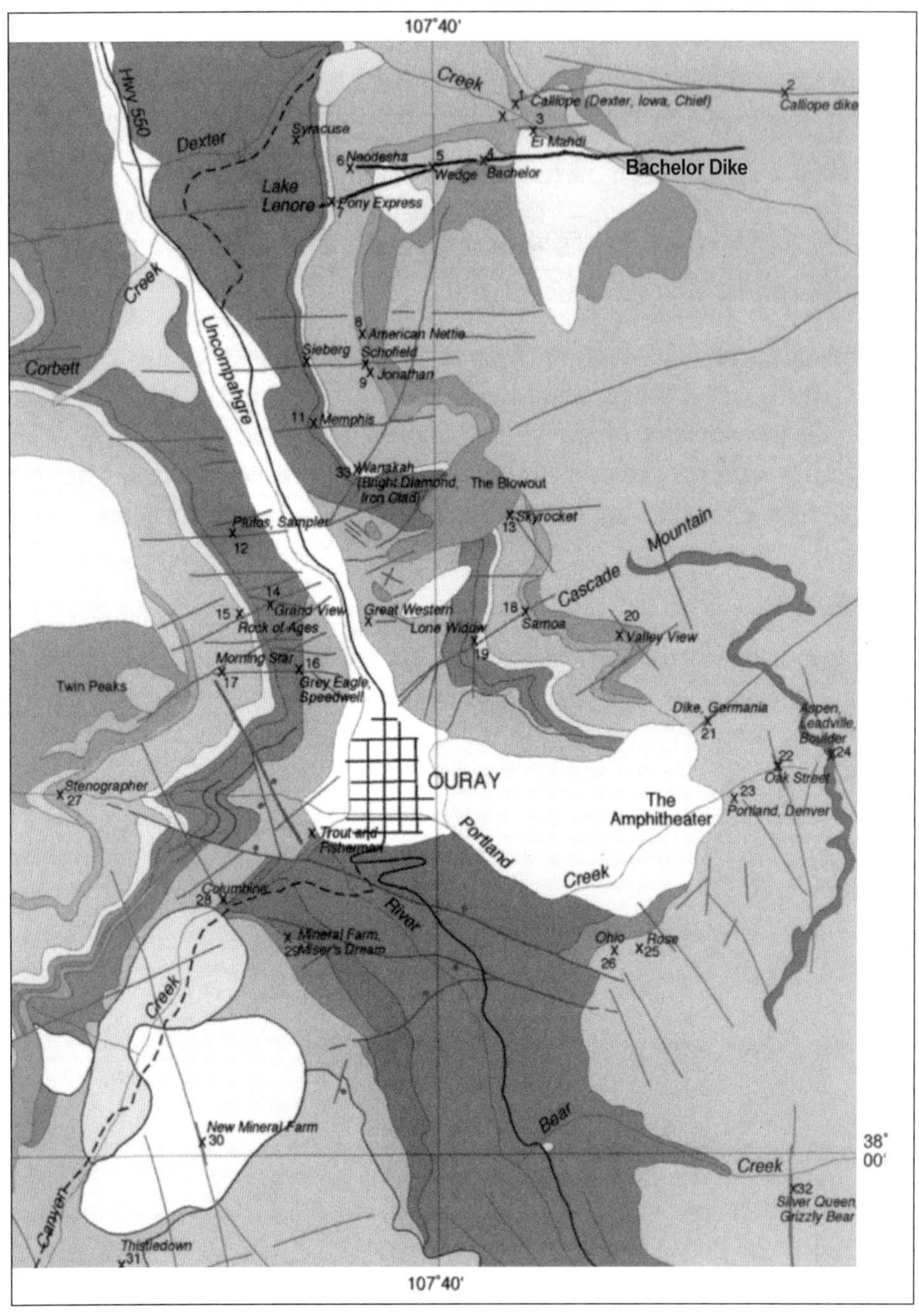

Geology and mines of the Ouray area, adapted from Kelley, circa 1957, Luedke & Burbank, 1981. By George Moore as it appears in *Mines, Mountain Roads and Rocks*.

Ash, circa 1900. Khedive Portal is on the lower left connected to the mill (center of photo) by rail. Boardinghouse may be on the right. Houses are scattered up the hillside. Notice the piles of lumber in the foreground to be used at the mine.

(and relief, no doubt) for Ouray until the Camp Bird Mine started producing huge amounts of gold in 1897.

The greatest of all the silver mines on Gold Hill was the Bachelor Mine, and among all of the silver veins in the Ouray area it was one of the most economically important. The Bachelor vein was associated with the Bachelor Dike and was opened in three places; at the Bachelor tunnel on the south side of Dexter Creek, at the Wedge, and at the Neodosha, while the nearby Khedive, El Mahdi and Pony Express also had productive veins. When the Bachelor's location certificate was filed in 1888 it gave the Calliope as a reference point, since the Calliope was the most important thing in the neighborhood. But at 720 feet into the mountain, the Bachelor tunnel that had been driven 500 feet so painfully by Armstrong and Hurlburt suddenly intersected high-grade silver-bearing veins

Three horse teams (yes — count 'em) at Ash loaded with supplies for the mines. Circa 1900.
Ouray County Historical Society Collection

from two to twelve feet wide, and more than 4,500 feet in aggregate length. By 1907, ore valued at more than $2,000,000 came through the Bachelor portal.[10]

As the owners of the Calliope had done, Armstrong, Sanders and Hurlburt began to consolidate the mines on the south side of Red Canyon Creek into a mining group: the Bachelor Group. Legal problems flared with a few of the neighbors, and it wasn't until 1908 that things got ironed out. In the end, the Bachelor Group came to include seventeen patented mining claims and seven unpatented claims[11] including the Bachelor, Bachelor Royal, Khedive, El Mahdi, Wedge, Aberdeen, Old Admonition, and the Dick Bland Lode. Two titans, the Calliope Group and the Bachelor Group, now faced each other across Red Canyon Creek with the American Nettie and another gold mine, the Wanaka, going great guns at the top of Gold Hill.

Gold Hill was jumping, but the road down to Ouray was still little better than a trail. It took half a day to get to town and it wasn't practical to commute from there to work at the mines, so it wasn't long before miners started building cabins along Red Canyon Creek below the Bachelor near the Calliope and the Khedive. Soon a community of about 200 had grown up and was known as Ash, a name formed from the first letters of Armstrong, Sanders and Hurlburt. In 1899, Ash got its own post office. It also sported a mill, a school, and a community band: the Bachelor Band.

Life in Ash was much like that in any of the other small mining communities around Ouray. A miner's work was hard and dangerous, but also filled with a strong camaraderie. It took a special kind of person to be a hard-rock miner, and it took a special kind of person to be a miner's wife. Each day, when she kissed her husband good-bye, she never knew if she would see him alive again. The rhythm of life was the rhythm of shift changes at the mine, accompanied by the sound of signal bells. One bell meant a lift full of miners was on its way up, and they'd be home soon. Two bells meant they were on their way down. Seven bells was a sound

Miner's wife and children in front of a board and batten cabin, Ouray County, Colorado. Two of the children are boys and ride a mule, the little girl and the mother stand on the porch holding hands. Source: Frank Pecchio, Ouray.

Denver Public Library, Western History Collection, X-61353

A little boy and girl fishing at Lake Lenore, circa 1900.

Ouray County Historical Society Collection

no one wanted to hear. That meant there had been an accident, and everyone waited breathlessly to find out who had been hurt, and how badly. Even if it wasn't *your* husband, son or father *this* time, that hardly mattered. Everyone felt the fear, and everyone felt the sorrow.

Money was also a worry. Miners made a living, but they didn't get rich. At times, much ingenuity went into keeping food on the table. Sometimes families went mushroom-picking, and ate mushrooms instead of meat. Wild asparagus grew on the ditch banks, as it still does. Fish and game were available, although heavy hunting had reduced their numbers. Barter was very important: one lady might have received a big bag of potatoes or onions from family down the valley — another might have made more jam than her family could use. Neighborly trading of commodities made everyone's life richer. Old-timers often speak of the sense of family that marked those small communities, united as they were by mutual aid, fears, joys, and mutual sorrows.

Meanwhile, the children had the mountains as their playground. Favorite games included mumblety peg and drive-a-pig-to-town. In the latter, kids would form two lines. The player would attempt to drive a tin can, by hitting it with a stick, straight down between the two rows, and the others tried to keep him from doing it. If he failed he had to pay some kind of a ridiculous forfeit. Nearly all kids learned to ride horses, and racing was one of their favorite sports. They'd race anyplace the terrain was favorable, whether on horses or any other kind of four-footed animal. Raspberry and chokecherry picking were favorite pastimes, but an excursion over Horsethief Trail was really a thrill. Horsethief was only passable in July or August when the snow melted. Often the trail was barely wide enough for a horse, and at the Bridge of Heaven sheer cliffs dropped away on both sides. They still do.

Baseball games, fairs and rodeos offered welcome opportunities for excursions. At the base of Dexter Creek was the railroad siding that became known as Bachelor Switch. A ride into Ouray from Bachelor Switch cost a nickel, but it made youngsters feel like a million dollars when they descended grandly at the depot. The railroad later tried to change the name of Bachelor Switch to Lotus, but it

Miners pose with shovels between a Rio Grande Southern (RGS) boxcar and a mine building in Ouray County, Colorado (possibly Bachelor Switch). Circa, 1885. Source: Frank Pecchio, Ouray.

Denver Public Library, Western History Collection, X-61112

Miners pose outdoors in their best clothes at a mine in Ouray County, Colorado. Snow covers the ground. Are they on their way to Lake Lenore? Circa 1890. Source: Grant U. Marcy, Ouray.
Denver Public Library, Western History Collection, X--61109

didn't work. Perhaps it's a measure of the fondness people had for the Bachelor, because they wouldn't use the new name. Nor was the siding known as Calliope Switch, or American Nettie Switch. It was Bachelor Switch, and that was that. The spring flowers there were said to be some of the most beautiful of all.

While there was much wholesome fun to be had on Gold Hill, there was also another kind. Around the turn of the century, one of the toughest dance hall owners in Ouray, a man named George Wettengel, found it expedient to relocate to a healthier climate outside the city limits. Wettengel was a nephew of one of Ouray's founders, Gus Begole, but he "fell into bad company" and ended up running one of the most notorious houses in the red-light district on Second Street.[12]

Wettengel noticed there were a lot of miners making good wages on Gold Hill. He decided to make their lives easier by bringing the city's amusements to them, saving them the trip to town. Accordingly, he set up shop on Gold Hill at Mannon's Lake. It seemed like a foolproof idea: liquor, music, fun-loving girls, moonlight on the water, conveniently located near the mines....

To help publicize the place, Wettengel renamed the lake after one of his most popular girls, Lenore, and Lake Lenore it is to this day. But one of his other best girls, Julia, became jealous and angry over this favoritism. According to local legend, Wettengel married her to soothe her hurt feelings. History does not record which of the two women felt she got the better deal.

Although the "sporting house" at Lake Lenore began well, it wasn't as successful as Wettengel had hoped. Lenore left for greener pastures, and after a few years Wettengel abandoned the place. He even turned over a new leaf. He and Julia moved back to Ouray where they became solid citizens: he a legitimate business-man, she a housewife.

As the couple grew older, Julia became ill. Wettengel nursed her faithfully until, at the age of 59, she died. Her husband erected a handsome granite head-stone at her grave in Cedar Hill Cemetery. Then he really astonished the good people of Ouray.

Every day for the next fifteen years Wettengel walked five miles each way to the cemetery, during all but the dead of winter, to visit Julia's grave. Even in the winter

Skating party, Lake Lenore, circa 1890. Could the white, two-story building in the background be the "Sporting House?" Notice the lack of trees; timber had been cut for the mines.

Wettengel tombstone, Cedar Hill
Cemetery, Ouray, Colorado

© Louis Duke

he still made it at least three times a week, so the old-timers said. It was only when he was a few days away from his own death that he finally stopped going. He lies in an unmarked grave at Cedar Hill, beside his Julia.[13]

As the 20th century dawned, the light was dimming for the mines on Gold Hill. The richer, more easy-to-get-at ore had been removed first. That left ore of declining quality that required more and more money to extract. The outbreak of World War I halted the flow of money from British investors, always an important source of funds for the mines around Ouray. A generation of young men went off to war, and those who came back found the world they'd known had changed forever. The miner was now a replaceable part in an industrial machine. Mining had lost much of its sense of adventure and rugged individualism to consolidation and corporate control.[14] The small, independent operations talked about in the Windham report had become almost as rare as dinosaurs. It seemed only large corporations with huge economies of scale could make it. In December of 1905, the post office closed at Ash. In 1928 Dexter Creek flooded violently, tearing out most of what was left. Eyewitness Pearl Hopkins said the creek, normally only a few feet deep, ran 100 feet deep on that day.[15] The town was not rebuilt, though its remains still straddle Dexter Creek.

World War I brought the end of an era in many ways. Much ore still remained in Gold Hill, but it became increasingly hard to make it pay. In the 1920s Charley Armstrong even tried to find new ore at the Bachelor using a dowsing wand. No large bodies of ore were found, but the Bachelor was far from finished. The Syracuse Tunnel would see to that.

Tale Three – The Mine
A Shot in the Dark

One could say the Bachelor Mine was a shot in the dark. Ordinarily, the way to find a mining claim was to look on the surface for an outcropping of ore — but the Bachelor didn't have an outcropping.[1] What it did have was George Hurlburt and Charley Armstrong.

Hurlburt, having surveyed most of the mines on Dexter Creek, was privy to information that most men didn't have. Armstrong was an experienced prospector of more than average ingenuity. Together they might have been able to see the big picture on Dexter Creek better than most, but still, they didn't have x-ray vision. It was no small act of bravery to punch a hole in Gold Hill and hope to hit something, but that's just what they did.

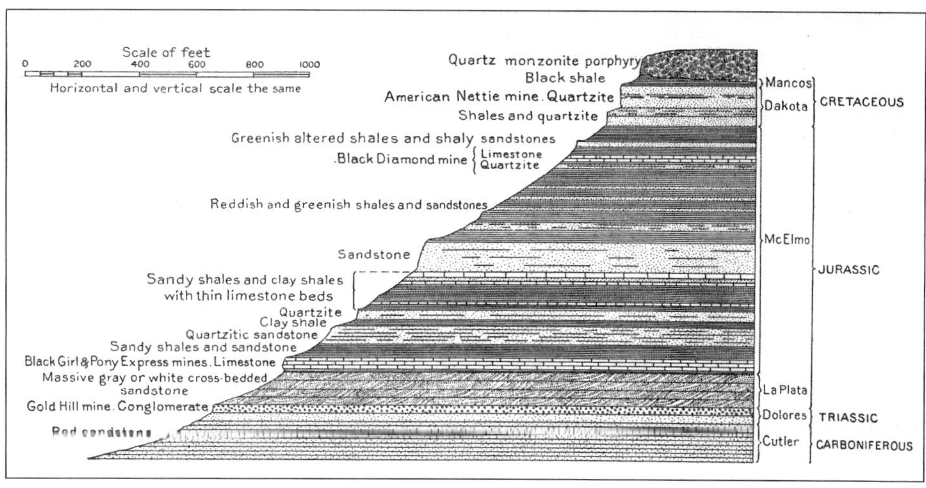

Geological section of Gold Hill

Geologic Atlas of the United States. Ouray Folio. Colorado. No. 153. U.S. Geological Survey Washington DC 1907. S.J. Kubel, Chief Engraver. Used under public domain fair use policy

As it turned out, they were wrong. They intended to hit the El Mahdi vein, but it was not the El Mahdi they hit. Instead, they hit a vein linked to what came to be known as the Bachelor Clastic Dike.

When the Bachelor Dike was rammed through the mountain by the Earth's explosive forces, the rock through which it passed was naturally fractured and deformed. This provided passages for mineralizing solutions that later came percolating upward. Sometimes the solutions congregated on one side of the dike, but sometimes they passed through it and continued on the other side. The solutions might squeeze into thin cracks, or find larger pockets in which to deposit their minerals. They may have even enlarged spaces for themselves by dissolving the surrounding rock. Sometimes, later fracturing made it so convenient for the mineralizing solutions that they replaced the whole width of the dike and left the country rock alone on either side.[2] They also might leave the dike and flow out between layers of rock in one direction or another as opportunity arose,[3] but it was the dike that prepared the way for them and maximized their chances.

In the Bachelor's case, the country rock around the dike is sedimentary layers of the Mancos and Dakota Cretaceous formations and the McElmo series of the Jurassic (now known as the Morrison Formation).[4] According to Carl F. Dismant, the current owner of the Bachelor, there are clues when one is getting

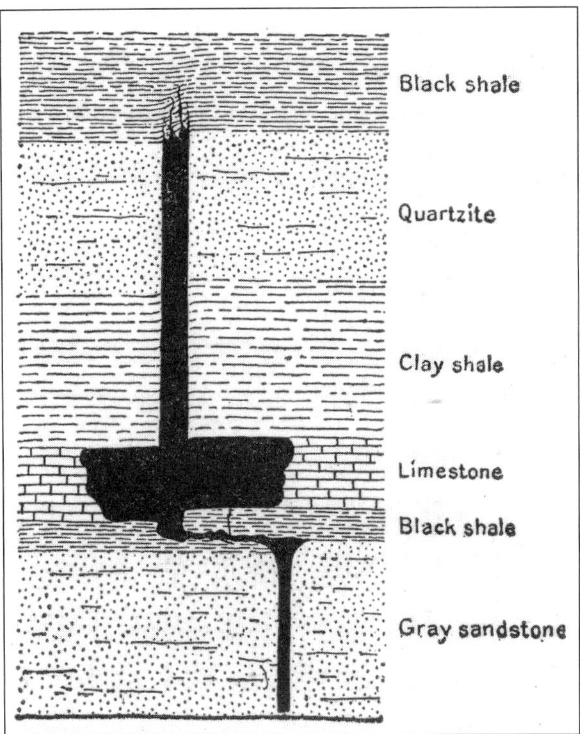

Type of silver-bearing vein, modified by replacement and bedding fault.

Illustration by T.A. Rickard in Across the San Juan Mountains, *1907*

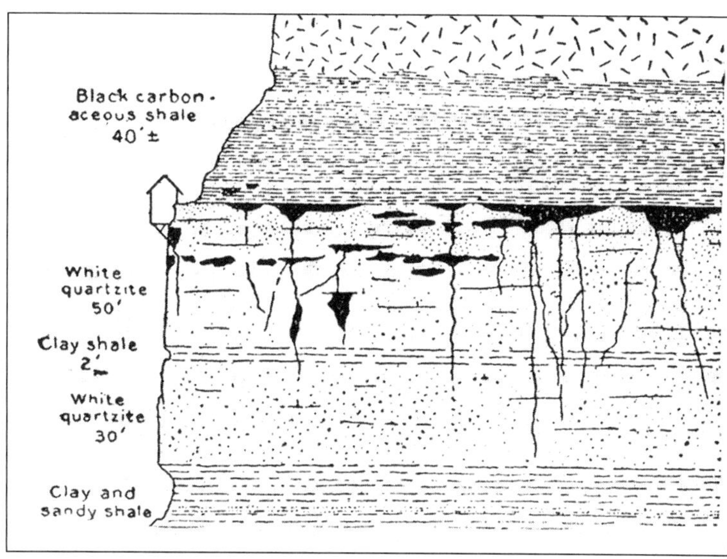

Section of American Nettie ore bodies

After J.D. Irving, U.S. Geological Survey. From T.A. Rickard in Across the San Juan Mountains, *1907*

close to the dike. The rock there is very hard, with peculiar narrow black horizontal stringers of silver. The dike itself is usually three or four feet wide, but that can vary greatly. A primary characteristic of the dike is the pronounced arrangement of the clastic rock fragments with their long axes parallel to the wall of the dike. This arrangement is especially obvious close to the walls, which form a definite parting from the country rock.[5]

Under magnification, the parallel rock fragments look like trees felled by some great blast — an atomic bomb or the Mt. Saint Helen explosion — all lying parallel with their tips pointing in the same direction. How exactly the Bachelor Dike was formed has been hotly debated by geologists for the last hundred years, and the debate promises to go on for another hundred.

In general, the ore-bearing veins on Gold Hill run east and west, with the most productive veins being the ones south of Dexter Creek. In those mines, the ore shoots tend to reverse from their normal dip toward the northeast because of a flexture, possibly caused by slumping toward the mountain's front. It seems the additional cracking along this flexture may have provided especially welcoming places for minerals to form, since the Pony Express, Bachelor and Calliope all show especially strong ore in that area.[6] If, however, the mineral solutions came to a relatively nonporous layer such as shale, their upward progress was arrested and they tended to spread out sideways, if they could, in fissures between the layers of rock. These flat sheets, called "rolls," can extend ten to forty feet out from the main vein, but in the Bachelor they extended continuously for much farther than that. If the beds were flexed, as just described, there was even more room for ore to form and the rolls could become quite wide.[7]

It was one of these wide rolls that made Armstrong, Sanders and Hurlburt rich; but the date is hard to determine. We know the original location certificate on the Bachelor was filed in 1888.[8] We know Armstrong started work on a tunnel; or more properly a "drift," since a tunnel is open at both ends and a drift is not. Local legend says that the drift was 500 feet into the mountain when Armstrong and Hurlburt ran out of money and brought Sanders in. The record shows that the vein was struck at 720 feet.[9] It shows that Sanders bought Alf Armstrong's one-third interest in the mine on November 28, 1894 for $2,000,[10] and by 1895 the Bachelor was the top producer in the area.[11] Various sources place the date of the big strike anywhere from 1889 to 1895. Armstrong's obituary in the *Ouray Herald* placed it in 1892.[12] Hurlburt's obituary in the *Herald* placed it in 1893.[13]

Why Sanders paid $1,900 more than the going rate to buy his one-third interest in the mine remains unknown. And if it was worth that much, why did Alf want to sell? It may be that Alf had lost interest in the mine, even though it did look promising. Ouray County records show that he bought and sold quite a bit of real estate in Ouray. Perhaps he was more of a wheeler-dealer than a miner, and decided to take his money out of the Bachelor to use in one of his other schemes.

Whatever the case, it is clear that the Silver Crash of 1893 significantly reduced the Bachelor's early returns. The ore was a high-grade silver ore with pockets of ruby silver that were said to have contained 15,000 ounces per ton, together with small amounts of gold.[14] The vein, from two to twelve feet wide in places, was worked for 1,000 feet to the east, and to the west it connected with the workings of the Wedge and the Neodosha. At the Wedge the vein forked, and the two branches were separated by an interval of about 200 feet.

By 1905, the Bachelor had produced between $1 million and $2 million dollars worth of ore.[15] Had silver not lost twenty-five percent of its value after the Silver Crash of '93, the total would have been much higher. Nevertheless, $2 million would be worth more than $37 million today... still a tidy sum.

Left: View west on Eighth (8th) Avenue, Ouray, Colorado, of a street crowded with teams of horses and mules hitched to wagons loaded for the mines. The Denver & Rio Grande Railroad depot and train depot and trains show across the Uncompahgre River in distance. 1892. Source: Ross Beaber.

Denver Public Library, Western History Collection, X-12822

An ore wagon loaded with high-grade ore and pulled by a six horse team ready to head down to town. Behind it, miners' houses and a shop building with barrels on the dock. Source: Walker Art Studios Montrose, Colo.

Denver Public Library, Western History Collection, X-62041

The Bachelor workings increased steadily during the 1890s and through the turn of the century. Other mines were accessed and became involved in the Bachelor's underground network. One, the Khedive, was subsequently enlarged by 4,000 feet to the east and 2,000 feet to the west. According to Dismant, a lot of money was made when 200 feet of good ore was discovered right where the Bachelor met the Khedive.

For a while, the Bachelor's ore was so rich it could be shipped straight to the smelter in Leadville without any processing other than sorting. Over time, however, the quality of the ore began to fall as the richest ore was shipped away. Sometime around 1900, Hurlburt and Sanders decided they wanted out, and sold their interest in the Bachelor Group to Charley Armstrong. Armstrong then proceeded to do what many mine owners did to try and increase profits: he built a mill near the mine to process the lower quality ore.

Ash in the winter. Building in the center is probably the Bachelor Boardinghouse.

Ouray County Historical Society Collection

Gray copper, also called tetrahedrite, gave the miners on Gold Hill an especially hard time. Tetrahedrite from the Bachelor typically contained sixty ounces of silver to the ton, but getting the silver out of the rock was very difficult. In processing, it tended to form slime that was very hard to work with and, as a result, much of the value was lost. Shipping the ore to the smelter in Leadville was expensive, too. The Bachelor's ore was, and is, refractory ore containing large amounts of lead, silver, zinc and copper, as well as gold. "Refractory" means obstinate, difficult to melt, and resistant to heat. It takes a great deal of heat to remove the valuable minerals from refractory ore. That means specialized facilities, and that means more expense.

Not only was the Bachelor running out of high-grade ore, but the wider veins had been cleaned out. There was still ore of respectable value, but it was found in much narrower veins. To mine those narrow veins economically, huge dynamite blasts were out of the question: they would produce too much waste rock in addition to the ore. Greater precision was needed to mine the ore cleanly.

Enter, the Tyrolean miner. Although some Austrians and Italians had come to Ouray earlier, the 1890s saw the arrival of many more. Usually, they were from the mountainous parts of western Austria and northern Italy next to Switzerland: a region known generally by its Austrian name, Tyrolia. The San Juans were much like their homeland. Not only were they experienced in hard-rock mining, but some had done coal mining that required them to work carefully in very small spaces. They were, therefore, especially good at working the Bachelor's narrowing veins. Many times they worked alone, far back in the rock with just enough space to accommodate the movements of their elbows. Claustrophobia and, in fact, fear of any kind must have been unknown to them. The Bachelor made good money for a number of them, who were said to have returned home to Italy as wealthy men. More about the Tyrolians later.

Two miners working by candlelight tend a diamond drill rig one mile underground in a mine near Ouray Colorado. Circa 1885.

Denver Public Library, Western History Collection, X-61079

A miner wearing a leather apron poses with his cat near a mine operation in Ouray County, Colorado. Four miners pose near the shafthouse.

Denver Public Library, Western History Collection, X-61975

The Tyrolians helped extend the Bachelor's initial heyday but then World War I broke out, and working men of every nationality disappeared into the military. When they returned — those who did return — they were further decimated by the terrible Spanish Flu epidemic of 1918. Whether because of the cramped quarters they worked in or for some other reason, the epidemic is said to have hit the miners especially hard. Coffins were piled up at the Ouray depot, waiting for the train to take the dead home for burial.[16] Short of experienced miners and unable to find significant new ore, Charley Armstrong was forced to sell the Bachelor.

The American Smelting and Refining Company (ASARCO) was the Bachelor's next owner. They sunk the 551-foot Bachelor shaft, directly connecting all of the Bachelor's nine levels. They also drove the Bachelor 350 feet east and 2,000 feet west, unearthing about 21,000 ounces of silver, aggregate.[17] In spite of its convenience, however, the Bachelor shaft also made the mine a more dangerous place, as falls were the most common cause of death in a mine. When exhausted, sweaty miners were hauled swiftly up into cool air, they could become faint. If they fell from the lift, their bodies might ricochet down the shaft and be torn apart by repeated impacts on rock walls and timbers until nothing but a rain of small fragments reached the bottom.[18]

Even when safety cages with emergency brakes replaced the older hoist buckets miners still died in lift accidents. Five of them died at the Virginius Mine in December of 1896 when a cage fell 1,100 feet in the Virginius shaft.[19] Besides the additional danger, the Bachelor shaft had another problem — it soon began to resemble a water well. Water poured out of the mountain, collecting in the shaft. It had to be pumped constantly, straight up. Ore had to be lifted the same way, and the expense of fighting gravity ate into the company's profits. After a few years they quit, and the shaft quickly filled with water.

Meanwhile, at a mine called the Mountaintop, general manager George Beebe was not a happy man. The Mountaintop was having all kinds of trouble, including labor trouble, and Beebe wanted to make a fresh start. He and Ouray mining promoter John Zanett decided to acquire the Bachelor and form the Bachelor Consolidated Mining Company. World War I had recently fueled a boom in strategic metals such as lead, zinc and copper, and that got Beebe to thinking.

Just before ASARCO pulled out of the Bachelor, it was said they had found a huge body of ore at the bottom of the now-flooded shaft. What if Bachelor

Both pages; The men of the Bachelor Mine (cover photo) pose with their dogs at the mine. Circa 1890. Source: Rosenstock '56.

Denver Public Library, Western History Collection, X-61106

Consolidated drove a drift into the side of Gold Hill and pierced the shaft? They could: a) drain the shaft and, indeed, the whole mine; b) provide natural, non-mechanical air ventilation through the mine; c) access the "huge body of ore," whatever it was, and; d) remove it, and any other ore they might find, on a gently downward-sloping track with gravity as their friend instead of their enemy. It was a good plan.

It would seem that Ouray was in need of a good plan. In spite of its upbeat tone, this year-end review of Ouray County's mining activity sounded a little hollow. "At the close of the year of 1924, but one property was working, and that was the Bachelor Consolidated, Manager George H. Beebe having just returned from the East, where he had interested his Eastern friends in investing funds for the development of the Bachelor property," reported the *Ouray Herald & Plaindealer*.[20]

Beebe's Eastern friends included a group of investors from Syracuse, New York, who put up most of the money for the project that became known as the Syracuse Tunnel. Work officially began on Christmas Day, 1924,[21] which is surprising because the mines were customarily idle only two days a year: Christmas and the Fourth of July. Somebody must have really wanted to get started. Although mechanical drills were in use by that time, to save money the Syracuse drift was driven the old-fashioned way: with heavy hammers and hand steel drills.

On the way to intersection with the shaft, Bachelor Consolidated hoped to find a suspected intersection of the Bachelor and Pony Express veins. That didn't happen, but still, much excitement was generated when miners found a vein of good ore three feet wide. "It is merely a question of a short time until the Bachelor property is again one of the big producing mines of the San Juans,"[22] said the *Herald & Plaindealer*. The tunnel reached the shaft in June of 1927. It was 5,000 feet long, and only off target by half an inch.[23]

As the tunnel drew close to the shaft, so much water had already drained from it into the tunnel through crevices and veins that crew boss Jesse Steele announced the shaft was dry.[24] However, according to local legend, an estimated two million gallons of water were still waiting in the Bachelor shaft. When the final rounds

Left: Miners inside a mine building in Ouray County, Colorado. Pieces of ore litter the floor. The man in the middle holds a singlejack hammer. Circa 1895. Source: Frank Pecchio, Ouray.
Denver Public Library, Western History Collection, X-61113

went off, the resulting plume of water arched from the portal like a fire hydrant, washing ore cars and all into Lake Lenore.[25]

Once the drift was cleaned out and readied for production, the huge body of mystery ore was discovered to be manganese. Black as sin and heavier than a guilty conscience, the manganese was in fact a potentially valuable ore; but according to Dismant this particular ore is so peculiar in its composition that no one has yet figured out how to process it. Nevertheless, good silver ore also had been discovered, and all the other objectives of the project were achieved. Beebe had exhausted his resources and retired from the area.

The Bachelor became one of the most desirable mines to work in. The road had improved, and it wasn't too far from town. It was free from snow slides, and it had good air. Not only was there now natural ventilation but all the machines at the Bachelor were run on compressed air, and that meant freedom from exhaust fumes in the mine. The new boardinghouse was comfortable and its food had a good reputation — always a top priority for the miners. One reason why the old boardinghouse and the town of Ash were not rebuilt after the 1928 flood was that the focus of operations had now moved to the Syracuse portal. The Bachelor may not have recaptured its former glory, but it was still a producer.

Beebe wasn't the only one with friends in mining circles. John Zanett, who became the patriarch of a very prominent Ouray mining family, had friends of his own. One was G.A. Franz, of St. Louis. Zanett's enthusiasm about Ouray and the San Juans came to infect Franz, and he in turn interested a group of St. Louis investors. In the late 1920s Franz moved with his family to Ouray and organized the Banner American Mining Company. Locals said the alternate meaning of the acronym B.A.M. was Burroughs Adding Machine Company, because that's where they believed the investment money had come from.

Whatever the case, Banner American built a large mill on a ledge southwest of Lake Lenore, leased several mines to provide ore and bought the Pony Express outright.[26] They also intended to do custom milling for mines throughout the region.

According to John Zanett's grandson, Dick, G.A Franz and his investors spent $5 million developing properties throughout the San Juans. When the Great Depression hit in 1929, Franz and Zanett made a conscious decision to keep both the Bachelor Mine and the Banner American Mill open.[27] For that, many of the

Above: The Ash complex in 1900

Ouray County Historical Society Collection

Below: The same view as it appears today. The tailings pile in the center of the picture above is to the left in the photograph below. It's interesting to note how much the area has returned to its former state with little reclamation effort... of course, Dexter Creek helped.

© Louis Duke

In the early 1900s, Charley Armstrong bought his partners out and built a mill near the Bachelor Mine to treat lower-grade ore.

Ouray County Historical Society Collection

people of Ouray are still grateful. Very few mines were able to operate through the Depression. In those days, more men were employed by the Bachelor and Banner American than by the renowned Camp Bird.[28] Al Fedel, a life-long citizen of Ouray, said that — figuratively speaking — "men were lined up from the portal all the way down to the highway, waiting for someone to quit so they could get the job."[29] Others brought their lunch and waited all day every day in front of a garage at what is is now the Apteka pharmacy (just north of Sixth and Main) in case someone wanted to hire day laborers.

Mining had always had its ups and downs, though. For many mining families, the Depression was just one more of the downs. They dealt with it as they always had. "When times were hard we got along fine. We never had to go to the government for anything,"[30] said one proud Depression wife, and others have said the same.

Once again, barter and trading resources among families helped everyone stay afloat. Sometimes items of barter could be made out of unlikely materials. Not everyone refused government food aid. Lee Kloepfer, who grew up in Ouray during the Depression, had this story to tell. "The relief gave us grapefruit juice, so we had quite a bit on hand. Mom was always trying to think up some way to use it and came up with the idea of grapefruit meringue pies. They were great, since she made them the same way as lemon meringue pies."[31]

Technologically, time stood still at the Bachelor. All work was done by hand, because it was too expensive to turn on the giant air compressor. Nevertheless, the Bachelor stayed open and the Depression gradually began to loosen its grip. Not only did the Bachelor stay open, but sometimes fortune still smiled on it. In 1939 Frank Fedel leased the Bachelor. With his son, Al, and relatives John Rossi and Frank Piccata, he was said to have made $80,000 mining new ore there.

It was World War II that finally ended the Great Depression. Strategic metals were again in high demand, and so great was the need that draft deferments were available to men who would work in the mines. Julius Sonza, yet another son of northern Italy, had started work at the Bachelor under George Beebe. When the United States entered the war, Sonza leased the mine and obtained a federal government loan to produce base metals for the war effort. It was nip and tuck, though; the Bachelor's ore was almost too rich in silver to qualify for the loan. The government wasn't interested in silver. Base metals were what they wanted.

Remains of the Bachelor Mill at Ash as they appear today. Note that Dexter Creek took out the two lower levels of the mill. All that's left is the topmost level.

Some mines in the Ruby Trust basin south of Ouray were not able to qualify for government loans, for that very reason.

In the course of administering the loan, a consulting government engineer suggested to Sonza that he should extend the 200 level east, and then go up. After only forty-three feet, they hit a twelve-foot wide roll containing 5,000 tons of ore including 250,000 ounces of silver, 1,000 ounces of gold, 1 million pounds of lead, 2 million pounds of zinc, and 50,000 pounds of copper.[32] It was almost too much for Sonza, who was also extremely busy running a number of other businesses in Ouray at the time. Besides making money, Sonza also got an ulcer.

Banner American thought this was a good time to sell their holdings, and Sonza thought so too. The Bachelor Group and the Banner American Mill were bought by American Lead & Zinc. They had big plans for the Bachelor until the war ended, and the demand for strategic metals collapsed again. There was a resurgence of interest during the Korean War. Another federal loan was obtained, with some fairly good results, but when the Korean War ended the British Government dumped its reserves of lead and zinc and the price of those metals plummeted. American Lead & Zinc closed the Banner American mill, and the Bachelor couldn't afford to operate without the mill.

Carl I. Dismant (Father of Carl F. Dismant, the current owner) a mining engineer and friend of Julius Sonza liked the Bachelor, and after the war — when everyone's attention was on uranium — he was able to acquire the mine. Through the 1960s and '70s, the mine was leased by various hopefuls. According to Harry and Nick Peck, who worked on some of the upper levels, there were still some sizable pockets of ore to be found in the '60s. One day, the Pecks exposed a streak of ore two feet wide. "We thought we had it made," said Harry. With great excitement they drilled the holes to shoot another round, but when the smoke cleared they found... nothing. Mining is just like gambling in many ways, and hope springs eternal. The Pecks' enthusiasm was dampened for good, however, when they finally managed to amass a good volume of potentially valuable ore only to have it washed away by Dexter Creek during one of its periodic rampages.

John Dade had better luck in the late 1960s when he bravely put the tenth level under the mine, below the Syracuse Tunnel. According to Dick Zanett, Dade hit some "kidneys," or kidney-shaped pockets of ore that paid fairly well.

Men and women pose by the abandoned American Nettie mill near Ouray, Colorado.
Automobiles are parked nearby. Between 1910 and 1920. The complex is visible from
U.S. Highway 550 on the west side of the Uncompahgre River.

Denver Public Library, Western History Collection, X-61998

However, the tenth level had to be pumped and there was no way to drain it, so Dade quit while he was ahead.

In the 1980s the silver market experienced a bubble, fueled by speculation on the part of the sensational Hunt family, of Texas. The same company that owned the Camp Bird leased the Bachelor, did $970,000 worth of work inside, and re-worked the dumps with a thirty-two percent recovery rate. Then the bubble burst, and in 1988 the Camp Bird Company gave the lease back to Dismant.

But in the summer of 1982 something new began at the Bachelor, when current owner Carl F. Dismant inaugurated tours of the Syracuse Tunnel in partnership with local businessman Tom Hash. Active mining was still going on at night, while tours were conducted during the day. No active mining is going on at present, but it could be with a mere thirty day start-up period, and the tours have proven to be very popular.

The Langos family enjoy the mine tour.
© Louis Duke

One of the things that makes the Bachelor/Syracuse Mine tour so popular is that it looks the way a mine of the Old West ought to look: exciting and mysterious. No sanitized amusement park ride, the Bachelor/Syracuse looks like the real thing because it is the real thing. Visitors ride 3,350 feet on the same tram the miners did, to a work station deep in the mountain. There, they see the silver vein and the ore chutes, and are treated to demonstrations of "hand-steeling" and other 19th-century mining technology. On the way out, many visitors gain a new appreciation for the welcome sight of "the light at the end of the tunnel."

Mysteries really do still remain in the Bachelor. So extensive are its workings that no one really knows for sure how many miles of them there are. There are rumors of a drift with fabulous ore that was purposely blasted shut, hidden for a more opportune moment, its exact location long forgotten. The Bachelor is still a relatively low-tech mine; but not only does that give the mine its special appeal, it also makes it possible for a small operator to succeed there. While it may be true that mining lost much of its romance and rugged individualism after World War I, that's not true at the Bachelor. There, the spirit of the frontier miner lives on.

Tale Four – The Miners
A Breed Apart

The following old joke speaks volumes about the miner's psychology. It goes like this:

One day, a miner died and was somewhat surprised to find himself standing at the Pearly Gates.

"Name?" asked St. Peter. The miner told his name.

"Occupation?" St. Peter asked. "Miner," the miner replied.

St. Peter consulted his book. After a few minutes of flipping back and forth through the pages, St. Peter began to frown. "I'm sorry," he said. "We've got all the miners we can handle. I'm afraid you'll have to go to Hell."

"What if some of the other miners left? Would that make room for me?" the miner asked.

St. Peter laughed. "That's impossible," he said. "No one would leave Heaven once they knew what it was like."

"If you'll let me in for just one hour, I'm sure I can persuade some to leave," said the miner. St. Peter looked at him incredulously.

"I don't suppose one hour will make much difference compared to eternity — but only one hour," St. Peter cautioned, and the Pearly Gates swung open.

About ten minutes after the miner was inside, sure enough, miners began to leave Heaven. Not only that, they seemed to be in a big hurry, jumping from the clouds and hurtling down into the dark depths toward Hell. The trickle soon became a flood and before the hour was up, the miner was the only one of his profession still left in Heaven.

St. Peter was amazed. "How did you do that?" he asked the miner.

"Easy. I just started a rumor that there was a big gold strike in Hell." said the miner with a grin.

"Well, we certainly don't have too many miners now. You can stay," said St. Peter.

Heaven was wonderful. Every time St. Peter saw the miner, he seemed to be blissfully happy. So it came as a surprise when one day Peter saw the miner sneaking out of Heaven, seemingly on his way to the infernal regions.

"Why are you leaving?" St. Peter asked.

"There's a big gold strike in Hell," the miner answered, looking sheepish.

"But that's just a rumor. You started it yourself!" St. Peter exclaimed.

"Yeah... but there just might be something to it," said the miner.

The siren song of hidden treasure calls to all of us. It's deep in our psyches. It's in the fairy tales we learned when we were still too little to talk. The difference is that miners are willing to endure much more and give up much more than the rest of us are to find it. And besides, they get to play with high explosives.

Few generalizations can be made about the San Juan miner. Because of its extreme physical demands mining favored the young, although it may have aged them quickly and made them appear older. Many certainly died young. One woman said she spent several years in Colorado before she saw a man with gray hair. But one of the founders of Ouray, Civil War veteran and prospector Milton Cline, already had gray hair when he came to the San Juans. He and other older citizens of early Ouray were affectionately called "Dad Cline," "Mother Cline," or "Dad Town" by one and all — a custom of the 1880s.

Even in the case of gender, it's dangerous to make assumptions about the San Juan miner. Although many miners did believe it was bad luck for a woman to enter a mine, the Señorita Mine on Gold Hill had a female owner and operator, Belle Hersinger.[1] Ouray County records show that as early as 1883 a woman named Kate Monroe started the Little Boston Mine near Red Mountain.[2] When ethnicity is added to the equation, things get even more complicated.

The first wave of prospectors to hit the San Juans were predominantly native-born Americans, many of whom were also born in the Territory of Colorado — children of the earlier mining boom that built Denver — while most of the rest hailed from the East and Midwest.[3] They tended to be placer miners. The word *placer* is Spanish and indicates a deposit of sand, dirt or clay, often in an active or ancient stream bed that contains fine particles of gold or silver.[4] The flakes of metal can either be panned from streams of water or washed from the hills using streams of water. Either way, it's a relatively easy technique that was favored during the earlier California and Colorado mining booms. The literal meaning of

San Juan miner in his cabin. Notice the "homey touches" of flowers, photos, tablecloth and books. "Pinups" and scenic photographs decorate the walls above his table. Circa 1890.

Denver Public Library, Western History Collection, X-61351

View of a placer mining operation, shows nozzles spraying water on a river bank, near Dallas, Ouray County, Colorado. This is the Dallas Creek Day Use Area of Ridgway State Park today.

Denver Public Library, Western History Collection, WHJ-663

placer is pleasure. But the silver and gold in the San Juans was not easy to get at. Instead, it required following veins of ore through some of the hardest, most obstinate rock on Earth.

British investment money arrived early in the San Juans, and the investors wanted to know their interests were in good hands. When it came to hard-rock mining, they knew no one had more experience than the people of Cornwall in southwestern England. The tin mines of Cornwall had been worked since prehistoric times. In fact, the need for the Britons' tin was one of the things that made Rome want to conquer them. So when English-backed mining companies needed hard-rock mining specialists, they looked to Cornwall.

Cornish miners who emigrated to the United States found work immediately. So good were they at their jobs that frequently they were asked if any more at home would like to come over. "Yes, I have a cousin Jack who might," was the usual answer. Eventually, all Cornishmen came to be called Cousin Jack, and their wives were Cousin Jenny. To this day, the heavy hammer used to drive drill steel is known as either a singlejack or a doublejack, depending on whether one or two men team up to use it, and the name of the modern reciprocating jackhammer still refers back to the Cornish miner, Cousin Jack.

Cornishmen were welcome in the San Juans, as they were everywhere, for their knowledge, amiability, and clever use of the English language. They tended to call everyone they talked to by some endearment, such as "my son," "my 'andsome," or "my beautay," and their wry sense of humor is legendary. When asked if he could suggest a good way to find gold, one Cousin Jack said, "Well, sorr, where gold is, it is, and where it ain't, there be I." Another, when asked during a court case whether there was an ore vein at the bottom of a certain shaft, said, "Not a dom bit, and smaller as 'ee goes down."[5]

From 1877 to 1880, it was mainly the Cornish miners who built St. John's Episcopal Church, one of the oldest permanent structures in Ouray. With its plain but beautifully made rock walls, St. John's looks much like a rustic English country church. Given the hard labor they performed daily, the Cornishmen must have very much wanted this reminder of home, because they built it in what little free time they had. Perhaps it helped with homesickness, or perhaps they did it out of devotion to their faith. The church is still very much in use, and is found at the

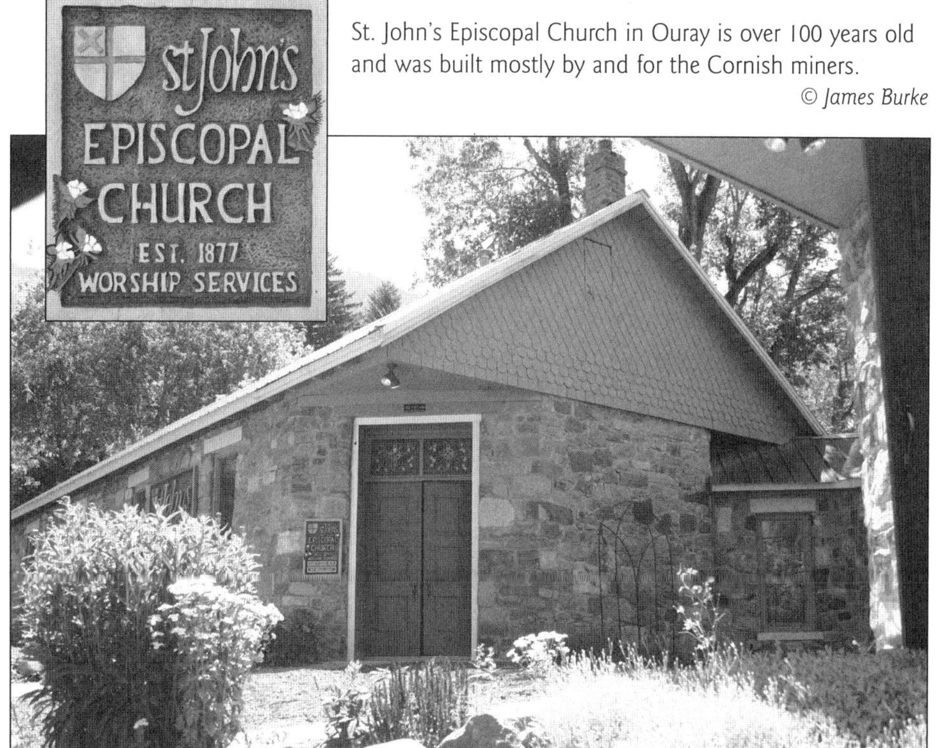

St. John's Episcopal Church in Ouray is over 100 years old and was built mostly by and for the Cornish miners.

© James Burke

corner of Fifth Avenue and Fourth Street across from the house that was for many years home to George and Cora Hurlburt.

The 1890s brought another wave of immigrants whose legacy lives on in Ouray. However, this one was driven by harsh necessity. Although they soon became experts at mining, the Tyrolians of northern Italy and western Austria didn't necessarily start out that way. Many were farmers, or skilled at the building trades such as carpentry and stonemasonry — trades that transferred well to the mines.

For hundreds of years, hostile armies swept back and forth through the alpine passes between Italy and the rest of Europe, wreaking havoc and suffering on the local populations. Tyrolia was extremely fertile both agriculturally and creatively speaking, which was good and bad since it made the area attractive to invaders. Not only did its people endure, however, they became tough, inventive and artistic, with rich local cultures and traditions. For a while, when it was part of the Venetian sphere of influence, both silk worm raising and silk textile production became important industries near the old Roman city of Tridentium, or Trent. Fruit growing and wine making were also traditionally important. Technologies and tradespeople passed easily between the Austrian and Italian parts of Tyrolia until it was hard to tell one population from the other, except by their dialects.

However, in the 1860s and through the '80s a series of catastrophes struck the region. First, a disease killed the silk worms, then another disease blighted the vineyards, followed by violent flooding. With the agriculture and textile industry reeling, the region was in no position to fight off trade competition from France. To make matters worse, in 1867 the Treaty of Vienna changed the borders of the Austrian Empire, making Trentino — the region around Trent — no longer a part of the empire. To try to get Trentino back on its feet economically, the Austrian government had been encouraging skilled Austrian workers to settle in northern Italy, but after the Treaty of Vienna the Austrians who had moved there found themselves culturally isolated.[6]

That was the last straw. Thousands of Tyrolians, both *Trentini* and Austrians emigrated in the 1880s and '90s, not only to North America, but to South America as well. Then in 1918, World War I ended with the Treaty of Versailles, which made Trentino officially a part of Italy. As Dominic Mattivi, who later settled in Ouray, told people, "One night I went to bed Austrian, and woke up Italian."[7]   Suddenly, German-speaking Tyrolians were required by their new

Miners pose on a mountain in Ouray County, Colorado. One man aims a rifle. Circa 1920. Source: Frank Pecchio, Ouray.

government to change their names and forbid their children to speak anything but Italian. The Tyrolians felt doubly isolated, and a new wave of immigrants left Trentino. Over time, they tended to reunite in mountainous regions similar to the ones they had left behind. Many of the best-known surnames in Ouray, such as Bonatti, Fedel, Fellin, Ficco, Leonardi, Mattivi, Rossi, Svaldi, Zadra, Zanella, Zanett, and Zanin arrived with the *Trentini*.

Silverton's Gerald Swanson, whose mother was from Trentino, characterizes the *Trentini* as industrious, thrifty, physically agile and practically fearless. Until the end of World War I the Italian-speaking *Trentini* arrived in the United States carrying Austrian passports — just one of the many contradictions that beset them. Many still considered themselves Austrian, though some did not. Immigration became a volatile issue in the San Juans during the 1890s because of fears over "cheap and foreign labor," and confrontations quickly took on ugly ethnic overtones. In his book, *Song of the Hammer and Drill*, Duane A. Smith gave the following example from the Lake City area, just over the range from Ouray.

> *A glimpse of events to come occurred at Henson, nestled beside the Ute and Ulay Mine. When the company required that single men board at the company boardinghouses in 1899, Italians working there refused to comply and marched out, but Americans tried to continue and were driven away. When Springfield rifles were stolen from the local armory and armed Italians seized the mine, the local sheriff called for Colorado National Guard troops. Ill will toward the Italians mounted and the troops arrived just in time to calm the situation in mid-March, though not before the local press cried that the "Italians must go." As a result of the uproar, the company agreed not to hire any more Italians, an injunction was issued to restrain the strikers, and the Italians were given a few days to leave the district.* [8]

Incidents such as that must have made the *Trentini* even more conflicted about their cultural identity. Arriving at New York's Ellis Island with Austrian passports, but speaking Italian, some *Trentini* refused to declare their nationality because they didn't want to be considered Italians.[9]

The hard life of the frontier took its toll on the hopeful immigrants from Trentino. Many young men died in the mines and young women were made old by unremitting work. The staple food, as it had been in the Old Country, was polenta. *Polenta* is boiled corn meal, cooked to such a consistency that when turned out of the pot it is thick enough to slice as it cools. Making polenta was a major kitchen ritual in Trentino households. It required an hour of almost constant stirring to be sure the polenta didn't scorch, while the batter got stiffer and harder to stir with each passing minute. Now, there's a workout.

Even the dietary habits of the *Trentini* had a split personality. According to Gemma Mattivi of Ouray, who came to the U.S. from Bedollo, Italy in 1949, a typical Trentino meal features polenta and sauerkraut.[10] Cross-cultural cuisine, to be sure. Gerald Swanson remembered the thing he heard most from his elders growing up was, "*Mangia! Mangia!* Eat! You'd eat it if you were in the Old Country, because that's all there was. You'd eat it or you'd starve!" said Swanson.[11] "We only had meat twice a year, at Easter and Christmas, in Trentino," said Mattivi.

Miners at a mine in Ouray County, Colorado. The men hold various tools that include planes, mallets, and saws. Circa 1885. Source: Rosenstock '56.

Denver Public Library, Western History Collection, X-61105

Immigration wasn't the only volatile issue in the San Juans as the 1800s drew to a close. Labor troubles of all kinds made headlines in the San Juans during the 1890s and early 1900s. As mining became less of an adventure and more of an industry run by corporate bean-counters with little or no understanding of what a miner's life was like, management's attitude toward the miners hardened. Mining engineer Thomas Rickard resigned as manager of the Yankee Girl Mine when the owners could only be convinced to pay their workers grudgingly. It was a common trick, he said, for companies to let the payroll fall in arrears, then close the mine, leaving the employees high and dry.[12]

Miners pose outdoors at a mine in Ouray County, Colorado. Snow covers the ground. Circa 1885. Source: Grant U Marcy- Ouray.

Denver Public Library, Western History Collection, X-61111

Scattered strikes hit the American Nettie over the price of board, the Guston in 1895 over wages, and the Revenue in 1896 over wages and the hiring of a shift boss, but in general the labor situation in Ouray County was substantially different from that of its turbulent neighbors. Undoubtedly, this was partly because of the leadership and decency shown by mine owners such as "The Gentleman," Charley Armstrong, George Hurlburt, and Tom Walsh. They provided their employees with exemplary working conditions, and the workers appreciated it. In his 1908 commencement address at the Colorado School of Mines, Walsh urged the graduates to treat miners with humanity and justice and to provide them with clean, comfortable quarters, wholesome food, and medicine. "To use a mining phrase, you will be prospecting in human hearts, and may discover beauties of character little suspected," he said.[13]

Even after Walsh sold the Camp Bird Mine to a group of British investors in 1902, his successors continued that philosophy. When the Camp Bird's general manager, John Hays Hammond, heard union miners from Telluride were coming to coerce his miners to strike, he called a meeting, discussed the issues, and was assured by his men that they would take care of the situation. According to Hammond, the confrontation between the union and his miners was brief. "You damn butchers, what are you doing here? Go back where you came from. You're going over the cliff quick if you don't get the hell out of here!" said the Camp Bird miners. The union men must have believed them. They left.[14]

Meanwhile, at the Bachelor Mine, there never was any suggestion of labor unrest. While not as plush as the Camp Bird, it did have the home life of Ash and the consolations of Lake Lenore close at hand, and contented workers don't strike. In addition to safe and humane working conditions, given the inherently dangerous nature of mining, one of the most important things a mine owner could do was to feed the miners well. From the very beginning, food carried a lot of meaning for miners and prospectors. They might endure incredible hardships and privation, but one of the things they wanted to do most when they got a chance was to eat the way they thought rich people ate.

Miners pose for a group portrait at a Ouray County mine. Notice cook in white apron on left. Circa 1895. Source: Henry W. Rathmell.

Denver Public Library, Western History Collection, N. H. Conley, X-62070

Loggers, cowboys, and other 19th century workers in dangerous occupations demanded good food as part of their wages, but among prospectors and miners, food had a special mystique.[15] The emphasis on food may have its roots in the prospector's original dream: to find hidden treasure and not just make a living, but get rich. Many experienced enough occasional windfalls to let them indulge their fantasies, if only for a little while. From its earliest days, Ouray's spicy newspaper *The Solid Muldoon* featured ads for champagne and oysters. That was before the railroad came, when items like those had to endure long, rough, hot trips over the mountains in freight wagons before reaching eager frontier gastronomes. In his fascinating book, *Bacon, Beans and Galantines*, Joseph Conlin outlined the situation this way.

> *Dining upon fancy "frenchy" or "keskydee" food was not only then emerging as an index of wealth and status in the United States, but it was also the one item in addition to warm baths, shaves, and whiskey that was immediately available in the diggings. One searches in vain among the few surviving inventories of the earliest ships to arrive (during the California Gold Rush) for the manifest of one crammed to the gunwales with champagne and canned lobster salad. But one cannot resist speculating that there was such a vessel and that her master got very rich.*
>
> *In every camp the experience of California was recapitulated, more quickly with each passing year: fabulous riches enjoyed by the discoverer and perhaps a few early comers; wide-open boom during which big money, at least in the form of claim certificates and mining stock, circulated freely; and only later consolidation of mineral holdings and reduction of the majority of the population to the status of wage workers who, however, were well paid and remained imbued with the habits of the first days.*
>
> *Among those habits was the yen for fancy eating and the belief, perhaps made more convincing by the monotonous food on long treks, that elegant meals were one way a rich man spent his riches.* [16]

There may also be physiological reasons why miners favored exotic foods, for miners consumed huge amounts of sugar, vinegar, pickles and salt. Gerald Swanson, who grew up around the mines in Silverton, speaks in his book *Swanee's Silverton* of how the older miners loved to drink the juice from sauerkraut.[17]

WILLIAM H. FAY.

FINE SOUR MASH

WHISKIES   **WHISKIES**

IMPORTED

LIQUORS   **WINES**   **CIGARS**

Mumm's Extra Dry, Piper Heidseeick, Dry Mono
pole, Imported and Native Sparkling and
Still Wines.

Anheuser and Ouray Beer on Draught

Bass and Ginger Ale, Porter, Stout, Appolonaris'
Geneva and London Dock Gins, Santa Cruz
and Medford Rums, Henessy BRANDY
CORDIALS, &c., &c.

SOLE AGENTS FOR THE

M. E. & M. E. Regalia Cigars.

Liquors by the Gallon, Quart, Pint or Flask.

FAMILIES SUPPLIED WITH ALL KINDS OF BOTTLED GOODS BY THE
BOTTLE OR CASE.

Cor. 6th Ave. and 3d St. Ouray, Colorado.

Ad for fine whiskey and champagne that appeared throughout the 1880s in *Solid Muldoon*, Ouray, Colorado

One woman who cooked as a girl for both loggers and miners said that "loggers would eat anything," but miners "had no appetite at all. The poison air ruined their stomachs as well as their lungs. It was hard to please miners. You had to wake them up with vinegar and lots of salty things."[18] Intense labor and the need to drink large amounts of water may have flushed the minerals out of a miner's system, while rock dust and powder smoke dulled the senses of taste and smell. According to Conlin, "the signal gastronomic difference between nineteenth century *haute cuisine* and the American fare on which the miners had been raised was the former's pungency.... It may be that the miners' fancy of such meals ought to be considered a vocational disease."[19]

Western Hotel, Ouray Colorado, today

© James Burke

With all the emphasis on savory foods, it's no wonder the grocery business was one of the best businesses to be in. Gus Begole, one of the original discoverers of gold in Ouray, immediately opened a grocery store. J. Frank Sanders, one of the three who made a mint out of the Bachelor Mine (and the only one to die wealthy) took his money off to Delta where he opened —

a grocery store. Julius Sonza, who also made a considerable amount of money from the Bachelor, still kept as one of his primary businesses a grocery store: the S & S Market on Main Street, where the Cascade Mercantile is now.

Another way miners and prospectors could indulge their fantasies of wealth was the class of ornate hotels known as the "miner's palace." The Western Hotel in Ouray is a classic example. With its fancy gingerbread architecture and comfortable bar — complete with richly appointed Victorian back bar — the Western told the miner that he was somebody who deserved to enjoy some of the finer things of life. If a miner could afford it, he might very well check into such a miner's palace for the winter and recoup his energy for next Spring's assault on the mountains. Fancy architecture was no guarantee of success, however. The reputation of the miner's palace rested squarely on its cuisine, and on delicacies the miners liked to think they could enjoy in common with Astors and Vanderbilts.

Cook at the Bachelor Mine
Denver Public Library,
Western History Collection,
X-61106

The mine boardinghouse, therefore, was in a sense judged by how its food compared with one of these miners palaces. The Bachelor boardinghouse compared well. When the new boardinghouse was built at the Syracuse tunnel, it had two of the best cooks in the area: Ami Massard and Mary Ficco. Massard was a Swiss chef and the father of Frank Massard, who for many years ran Ouray's Post Office Drug Store at the corner of Main and Seventh Avenue, and was one of the most beloved and most philanthropic citizens Ouray ever knew. When they were just boys, Al Fedel and Frank Massard would go up to the Bachelor boardinghouse to visit Frank's dad. They usually timed it to arrive for dinner. According to Al, they were careful to avoid arriving during the shift change, because that's when the miners would sort out all the "good-natured" pranks they played on each other, and "things could get pretty rough."[20]

Dining hall inside a mine's boardinghouse, Ouray County, Colorado. Notice how formally the tables are set with china dinnerware. Circa 1900. Source: Mabel Barbee Lee Photo Album 210 (C).

THE OURAY HERALD

Miners liked to play merciless practical jokes on each other. They would hide or blunt each other's tools and blame it on a mythical creature called the "stope ape." They would steal food from each other's lunches and blame it on the equally mythical "timber mice." They especially liked to play practical jokes on newcomers as a sort of test, or right of passage. According to Al Fedel, it was easy to tell who the new guys were — they were the ones with broken noses and broken hands because of drilling accidents.

John Crim, who worked at the Bachelor in the 1950s, remembered that Wert Kaufman was the hoist man then. He had an odd sense of humor, and liked to scare people. When the miners were in a hurry they might say, "Cut the rope, Wert," to indicate haste. Kaufman might respond by dropping them a suitable distance in the hoist, just for fun. Once at the work station, though, things were different. That was where the miner's money was made, and he was deadly serious about it. The time to blow off steam was either in the "dog house" waiting to go down, or in the hoist on the way up. Then the fellows might take it into their heads to wrestle a man to the floor, strip him naked and paint him all over with giant timber marking crayons, only to set him free when the hoist met the freezing weather at the surface.[21] The stress of working under conditions of great physical danger does odd things to a man, they say.

One of the most important men at the mine was the blacksmith. His primary job was to keep the drills sharp. It was a very demanding specialty that required much knowledge of practical metallurgy, not to mention psychology, to keep the miners satisfied. The blacksmith also made and maintained everything of metal in the mine, from hinges and pipe hangers to mule shoes. Among the *Trentini*, all blacksmiths went by the nickname of "Fabro." The root is the same one from which the word fabricate is derived: *fabricari*, which in Latin means to make or to build. Blacksmiths were a musical bunch, perhaps because of the rhythms of the bellows and the anvil that they worked with every day.

Left: Man working at an outdoor blacksmith shop. Shows an anvil, a bellows and a forge, pickaxes, hammers, and a woodpile. Notice the *Ouray Herald* newspaper on the ground. August 10, 1897. Collection Thomas M. McKee Collection. Source Source: T.J. McKee.
Denver Public Library, Western History Collection, Thomas Michael McKee, *Z-1262*

Miners sharpen drills with a sledge hammer and anvil in a mine shop, Ouray County, Colorado. Interior walls are hung with hoses and tools. Circa 1900. Source: Grant U. Marcy - Ouray.

Denver Public Library, Western History Collection, X-62023

Lathes and drill presses fill the interior of a machine shop at a Ouray County mine. Circa 1910. Source: Astoria Books.

Denver Public Library, Western History Collection, X-62024

Al Fedel said that the two blacksmiths he knew at the Bachelor, David Sentis and John Rossi, were always singing. He also said a good blacksmith didn't talk much while he was working. For one thing, it was hard to be heard over the roar of the fire and the ringing of the hammer. Instead, he would communicate with his assistant by tapping on the anvil in certain spots or with special rhythms. It was all part of the music of the forge. Carl Dismant remembered blacksmith Joe Crescenti who worked in the '50s keeping the giant air compressor going. "He could do incredible forge welding, and his tool sharpening was a work of art," said Dismant.

Another very important specialty was that of timber man. The timber man had the job of stabilizing the drifts and verticals, including the ones carrying the hoists and chutes, and building the staging on which miners stood when raising a shaft vertically. Like almost every other specialty, the miner's lives depended on the expertise of the timber man. Jack Clark, nephew of Julius Sonza, who worked at the Bachelor in the 1940s, remembered timber man Ole Hansen. Hansen was an expert at Old World craftsmanship, and was still making hand-hewn timbers for the Bachelor until Clark went away to World War II.[22] According to current owner Carl Dismant, some of the timbering done far back in the Bachelor demonstrates a level of craftsmanship that would be an ornament to any modern luxury log home.

Rigging the blasting caps and fuses on sticks of dynamite was another specialty that meant life and death to the miners. All in all, there were a hundred ways to be killed or maimed in a mine. But oddly, that was — and is — part of the attraction. It's been said that the imminence of death focuses the mind to a laser-like appreciation of being alive. Adrenaline is a very powerful drug and can be very addictive, as any extreme sports enthusiast can attest. Historian John S. Hittel wrote of the gold rush miner, "They were ready to go anywhere if there was a reasonable hope of rich diggings rather than submit to live without the high pay and excitement which they had enjoyed... many of them had become unfit for the placid and orderly routine...."[23] It's been said many times that facing death together — as in combat — produces a special kind of camaraderie that almost transcends any other kind of love. Add to that the tingle of anticipation a miner feels when setting off a round, waiting to see what the last blast may have uncovered, and the occasional thrill of actually finding hidden treasure, and it's no wonder mining "gets into your blood," as so many miners say.

Alfred Castner King or "Cassie," as he was known by many, was a young man working at the Bachelor when in March of 1900 the

Alfred Castner King, poet, was blinded by a premature explosion at the Bachelor Mine,

From Mountain Idylls and Other Poems *by Alfred Castner King, Fleming H. Revell Company, NY and London 1901*

premature explosion of a stick of dynamite killed his partner, and King was permanently blinded. In despair, King lay for months in various hospitals, hoping to regain even partial sight. But during this period of forced inactivity he slowly found scenes from his life in the San Juans forming vivid images in his mind. Far from letting his life be ruined, King became the poet laureate of the mines. For many years he toured the U.S. alone, reading his beautiful poetry to receptive audiences everywhere.

King's most ambitious epic was *The Passing of the Storm*, which he dedicated to the pioneer prospector. In his preface, he made some points about the San Juan miner that are frequently overlooked.

> *It has long been customary for writers of western fiction to picture this character as a large-hearted but rough and untutored individual, expressing himself in a vernacular consisting of equal parts of slang, profanity and questionable grammar, possessing no ambitions above the card table or the strong waters which cause all men to err who drink them. An intimate acquaintance with this class, extending from the years of infancy to middle age, convinces the writer that the common description is manifestly unjust and misleading.*
>
> *The men who flocked to the early gold excitements, and who subsequently prospected the western mountain ranges for their hidden wealth, were the cream of American and European manhood; men possessed of more than ordinary endowments of intellect, education and physique, while their industry, bravery and hardihood have never been questioned.*
>
> *Proof of this exists in the names which have lingered behind them as a matter of record, for it was the prospector who christened the mountains, gulches and mining locations of the west. A cursory perusal of the maps of mineral surveys in any western mining district will reveal in abundance such names as Hector, Ajax, Golden Fleece, Atlas, Pegasus, etc.; indicating that those who applied them were, if not college graduates, men not unfamiliar with the classics. The use of such names as Cleopatra, Crusader or Magna Charta, by a prospector unversed in history, would naturally be unexpected. One without knowledge of literature would hardly grace his location stakes with such names as Dante, Hamlet or Mephistopheles, while one entirely unlettered could not by chance hit upon such names as Pandora, Medusa or Sesostris.*[24]

Sneffels Range

© Roger Young

King's words bring to mind men like the genial Charles Armstrong, the admirable George Hurlburt, the generous J. Frank Sanders, and many other more recent mining gentlemen, who have left their communities richer in every sense of the word. Whether native-born or immigrant, the San Juans seem to attract men of courage and grace. As Alfred Castner King wrote:

> *The spirit of freedom is born of the mountains,*
> *In gorge and in cañon it hovers and dwells;*
> *Pervading the torrents and crystalline fountains,*
> *Which dash through the valleys and forest clad dells*
>
> *The spirit of freedom, so firm and impliant,*
> *Is borne on the breeze, whose invisible waves*
> *Descend from the mountain peaks, stern and defiant —*
> *Created for freemen, but never for slaves.*[25]

Tale Five – The Menagerie
Friends and Enemies

There was one class of miners that was not made up of free men, although they were professionals at what they did. Some of them worked all their lives in the mines and even went blind from the time they spent in the dark. Others, when they were finally given their freedom, had no higher ambition left than to scavenge in garbage dumps and hang around back doors waiting for a handout. Nonetheless, they did their job better than any man could do it, and although some may have been abused, many were warmly appreciated and even celebrated. They were the mules and burros of the mines.

Jackass Flats is the name of a wide ledge on Gold Hill, overlooking U.S. Highway 550 and Lake Lenore south of the Syracuse Tunnel. Roughly triangular

Lake Lenore, circa 1900. Jackass Flats is the rocky ledge above the lake.

Pack train led by a man in overalls on a horse; shows mules loaded with supplies and timbers headed for Gold Hill. Note the "Fox's Ear" peak in the background (top), a landmark on the "Amphitheater" near Ouray. Circa 1910. Collection L. C. McClure collection, 1890-1935; album III.

Denver Public Library, Western History Collection, Louis Charles McClure, G.H.A. Photo, MCC-3262

in shape, two of its sides are so high and steep that not even a burro would try to go down them. It made an easily-controlled area where the mules and burros could be turned out, and thus its name.

Drivers called mule skinners were in charge of the mules' care and performance. "The skinners were really good. They could talk to a mule and make it really seem to under-stand," remembered ex-miner Al Fedel. A mule could carry up to 500 pounds, but it had to be fed hay. Burros, on the other hand, could make do on what they could forage. They could

Patient and hardy, the burro held a special place in the hearts of miners.

Ouray County Historical Society Collection

only carry about 250 pounds, but they also had a shorter turning radius than a mule on extremely tight switchbacks. Local historian Roger Henn remembered what a spectacle it was in his youth when every morning a long line of pack burros left lower Main Street with supplies for the American Nettie and other mines on Gold Hill. Instead of taking the longer route up Dexter Creek, the burro train zigzagged right up the Blowout at an extremely steep grade.

In the mines themselves, mules were used to haul the heavy ore cars. If there were no mules, then the men had to push tram cars containing tons of ore all by themselves. In the Bachelor, tramming was done by either mules or humans through the 1940s. The miners naturally appreciated the mules that saved them so much work, and they tended to show their appreciation with treats. Woe to the man who approached a mine mule without carrots, apples or sugar in his pockets. If a mule came to expect such tribute as his due, he could do a very aggressive job of frisking the miner in search of it. And that's not to mention the volume of sound a disappointed mule can make in a stone chamber underground.

One of Gold Hill's legendary mules was named Queenie. She worked for years at several of the mines, and Queenie was a pro. She knew exactly where to stand to position her ore cars under the chute, and according to Al Fedel, Queenie could count. When the ore cars were full, and Queenie was told to start up, the linkage between each of the cars would make a metallic sound as it pulled tight. Queenie knew exactly how many "clinks" there ought to be and if there was one too many, she stopped immediately and refused to budge. Not only that, if she was especially peeved she kicked the first ore car off the track.[1]

Mules were not the only non-humans in the mine, however. Miners were also known to make pets of the rats that came to live in cracks and crannies. When the men would take out their lunches, good smells wafted through the mine. The rats came to investigate — their eyes glowing from dark corners, reflecting the miners' lights. No doubt they were often driven away, but rats can be very persistent. Some miners didn't mind them, and even fed them scraps from their lunches.

For the miners knew that as long as the rats were around, all was well. If the rats suddenly left, it meant something bad was going to happen — such as a cave-in or explosion. The miners had a saying: "When the rats move out, so does the miner." There were even cases of rats leading miners to safety, or warning of danger by pulling on the miners' clothes with their teeth.[2]

Miners seem to have been happy to see almost any other living creature in the lifeless world underground. Still, rodents in large numbers could be a real nuisance, eating the insulation off of electrical wires and causing all kinds of headaches.

Because of this, the miners sometimes made pets of ring-tailed cats.

White-throated wood rat, can get as big as 14 inches, although half of that is tail!

© Paul Berquiest

The ring-tailed cat isn't a cat at all but is related to the raccoon, sharing its bushy, black-banded tail. It is also called the "miner's pet" or the cacomistle, from the Mexican Nahuatil Indian word *tlacomiztli*, meaning "half mountain lion."[3] Not only did the ring-tailed cat keep the mouse population down, but it was especially sensitive to toxic gasses that might seep into the mine.

The ring-tailed cat, also called the "miner's pet.'
© Paul Berquiest

Unfortunately for the animal, the miner got his warning by seeing the cat become agitated and confused, followed by convulsions. Sometimes, as is well known, canaries were taken into mines for the same purpose. However, in the hard-rock mines of the San Juan Mountains, canaries were difficult to come by.

Another creature became an object of affection for at least one miner. Several of the miners who worked at the Bachelor in the 1950s remembered that hoist man Wert Kaufman was especially fond of bats. Naturally, one of the miners felt it necessary to gather up a number of live bats and put them secretly

Hoary bat. These little guys like to hibernate for short periods of time. They like mines because the temperature remains about stable in all seasons.
© Merlin D. Tuttle, Bat Conservation International.

in Kaufman's lunch pail. When Kaufman opened the lid, he was instantly engulfed by a small cloud of wildly flapping bats. Kaufman himself was unflappable, however. When Carl F. Dismant was just a boy, tagging to the mine with his father, he thought it was fun to disturb the bats and make them fly around. Kaufman was quite put out when the bats decided to take up residence someplace more quiet.[4]

There are also accounts of another kind of companion in the mines. This one wasn't human, but it wasn't an animal either. It was the Tommyknocker.

Belief in Tommyknockers arrived with the Cornish miners. Miners in many parts of Europe had a similar belief, although they called them by different names. Tommyknockers are thought of as small, gnome-like spirits that live underground. Like pixies, they can be helpful... but mostly they are mischievous. Their best-known way of communicating with humans is by tapping on the ribs of the mine. Sometimes, they might lead a miner to a rich body of ore with their tapping. Sometimes they just led him on a wild goose chase.

Another way a Tommyknocker might communicate with a miner in the old days was by blowing his candle out. If a miner's candle went out three times, superstition said he should leave the mine immediately. Maybe, it was a warning that there was going to be an accident, or possibly it was a warning of hanky-panky at home involving the miner's wife. Later, when candles were no longer in use, funny things could still happen to a miner's light. Nick Peck, who worked in the Bachelor in the 1960s, used to carry two lights at all times, just in case. Nevertheless, one of his most vivid memories of the Bachelor is the time he lost both of his lights, and had to find his way out in total darkness.

In 1895, the *Ouray Herald* had this story to tell.

The recent death of Alex Taylor at the Bachelor was attended by a curious circumstance. About three days before the fatality, Taylor went to work earlier than usual and when there was not a soul in the mine. When he came out he asked who had gone ahead of him into the mine. As no-one had been in, the miners made light of his story, which was as follows: "A man went ahead of me into the stope, stuck his candle into the wall and went to throwing down ore. Soon after he picked up a piece of rock and threw it, seemingly to attract my attention. The rock struck me on the brim of my cap in front and I spoke to the man but he did not answer."

Taylor insisted that the foregoing was absolutely true and could not be convinced otherwise. On the other hand it is positively known that there was no man in the mine. The foregoing coupled with the fact that Taylor had, of late, predicted that he was to be killed in the mine, is certainly strange to say the least. It is believed that men are sometimes warned of approaching death and this instance is in line therewith. Laying superstition aside, circumstances often play strange tricks.[5]

A search of the *Herald* failed to turn up Taylor's obituary. It is unknown how he met his death or whether he died at the Bachelor. From the tone of the *Herald's* story, it sounds like the circumstances of his death were assumed to be common knowledge among the paper's readers.

A hundred years later, long-time Syracuse Tunnel tour guide Louis Duke had this experience.

I was walking alone down the drift where it takes off toward the Pony Express when I heard three knocks within the rock on my right. It did not sound like rock hitting rock — it was very definitely a metallic sound just like a hammer hitting drill steel, and it was coming from inside the rock. Whatever it was, it made me want to be somewhere else in a hurry. It took me three years to go back there.[6]

Mysterious "Tommyknocker" visits the Bachelor/Syracuse...

Julius Sonza also saw odd things in the Bachelor, according to a story related by the current owner of the mine, Carl Dismant.

One night, Sonza was working late by himself in the Bachelor when far down the drift, toward the portal, he thought he saw a light flickering. Suddenly, it went out. Sonza thought he must have been mistaken, and went back to work.

A few minutes later, the light was back. It seemed to bob erratically about the tunnel for a few minutes, and then suddenly it went out. This time Sonza knew he'd seen something for sure.

This went on for some time. First the light would appear, bob about for a while, then suddenly go out. Sonza became increasingly concerned, because each time it appeared, the light came closer. He readied himself to confront whatever it was.

What it was, as it turned out, was Pete Boca. Pete was a notoriously hard drinker, who was hurrying to deliver a juicy piece of gossip he'd picked up in a bar that night to Sonza. Boca wore a miner's helmet with a light as he stumbled up the drift, feeling no pain. It was a good thing he wasn't feeling any pain, because he was so drunk he kept ricocheting off the ribs of the tunnel and falling down. That explained the erratic motion of the light, and its sudden disappearances.[7]

In the end, however, the miner's most implacable foe was not Tommyknockers. Nor was it cave-ins, falls or explosions. It was that deceptively innocent-looking creature, the marmot.

The marmot, or rock chuck, is sometimes called the "whistle pig" because of a warning whistle it gives to other marmots when it senses danger. A chubby, thickly furred rodent with short legs and a bushy tail, the marmot appears completely harmless. Its name is derived from the medieval Latin *mormotana*, or "mountain mouse." This "mouse" is more like a beaver in size, though, weighing in at about ten pounds. Over the years miners killed and

Marmot

© Roger Young

ate many marmots, especially when times were bad. The marmots took their revenge, however.

Marmots, like many other animals, crave salt, and they especially love the salt found in human sweat. At the mines, this salty goodness was frequently found on wooden objects like tool handles and, yes, toilet seats.

"We couldn't keep the marmots from eating the outhouse seats," said Al Fedel. "There'd be nothing but a big hole there. We'd lock up the out-house, and they'd still get in. We even tried painting the seats with glycerin sweat off the dynamite to poison them, but as far as we could tell we only killed one."

Marmot outside a mine in the San Juans. When the men and the mines are gone, the marmots will probably still be here.

© Brian Jacobs

"Marmots also loved anti-freeze from the engines of mine vehicles, but that didn't seem to kill them either," said Fedel. "They chewed through the hoses to get at it." In fact, they had a perverse need to chew every hose, belt and wire a vehicle possessed. "They ate everything out of every vehicle. Nothing but a shotgun would kill them. We took turns standing guard, but we couldn't keep that up forever. They'd actually fight over worn-out compressor belts that were thrown on the dump," Fedel said.[8]

After a hundred years of drama, romance and hardship, mining has almost ceased in the San Juans, for a number of reasons. But if the last vestige of this colorful era ever disappears from the mountains, the final victor and last one standing in this titanic struggle will — it seems — be the marmot.

Notes

CHAPTER 1

[1] Koch, David R., Curator, *George Hurlburt, The Life & Times of a San Juan Surveyor,* Ouray County Historical Society (Ouray Colo.; 1984), p. 1.

[2] Ibid.

[3] Rathmell, Ruth, *Of Record and Reminiscence* (North Suburban Printing & Publishing, Inc., Westminister Colo., 1976), pg. 56.

[4] Unpublished manuscript, "History of Ouray County," by Judge William Rathmell, 1940.

[5] Mining Deed Book 38, records of the Ouray County Clerk & Recorder, p. 161.

[6] Bowen, A.W., *Progressive Men of Western Colorado,* (A.W. Bowen & Co., Chicago IL, 1905), p. 360.

[7] Ibid.

[8] Unpublished manuscript, "History of Ouray County," by Judge William Rathmell, 1940, p. 22.

[9] *Delta County Independent,* August 7, 1895.

[10] Koch, David R., op. cit., p. 5.

[11] *Ouray Herald & Plaindealer,* October 26, 1924.

[12] *Ouray Herald & Plaindealer,* May 3, 1935.

[13] *Delta County Independent,* August 7, 1895.

[14] *Abstract of Testimony, John A. Thompson v. Thomas F. Walsh* (Douglas Taylor & Co., Law Printers, New York, 1905), p. 21.

[15] Gregory, Doris, ed., *Ouray County Cemeteries* (Cedar Hill Cemetery District, Ouray Colo., 1986), p. 6.

[16] *Ouray Herald & Plaindealer*, Feb. 17, 1921.

[17] *Ouray County Herald*, March 8, 1940.

[18] *The Solid Muldoon*, Feb. 29, 1884.

[19] Interview with Carl Dismant, May 30, 2005.

[20] *Ouray County Herald*, December 29, 1939.

[21] Gregory, Doris, *History of Ouray* (Cascade Publications, Ouray Colo., 1995), p. 279.

[22] Bowen, A.W., op. cit.

Chapter 2

[1] Burbank, W.S., *U.S. Dept. of the Interior Geological Survey Bulletin 906-E: Structural Control of Ore Deposition in the Uncompahgre District, Ouray County, Colorado* (United States Government Printing Office, Washington D.C., 1940), p. 191.

[2] Crum, Josie Moore, *Ouray County, Colorado* (San Juan History, Inc., Durango CO, no date given) pg. 19.

[3] Kushner, Ervan F., *A Guide to Mineral Collecting at Ouray Colorado* (Ervan F. Kushner Books, Paterson, New Jersey, 1973), p. 7.

[4] Hall, Frank, *History of the State of Colorado, Volume 4* (Blakely Printing Co., Chicago IL, 1889-1895, 4 Volumes), p. 251.

[5] Kushner, op. cit., p. 3.

[6] *Ouray Times*, August 11, 1877.

[7] Kushner, op. cit., p. 50.

[8] *The Solid Muldoon*, June 22, 1883.

[9] Wallace, Robert, *The Old West: The Miners* (Time-Life Books, Inc., Alexandria VA, 1976), p. 178.

[10] Kushner, op. cit., p. 64.

[11] Colorado Mining Assn. 1952 Year Book, p. 127.

[12] Unpublished manuscript, "History of Ouray County and Its Mines" by Frank A. Rice; Ouray, Colorado, 1961.

[13] Henn, Roger, *Lies, Lore and Legends of the San Juans*, (Western Reflections Publishing Co., Montrose Colo., 1999), p. 113.

[14] Smith, Duane A., *Song of the Hammer and Drill* (University Press of Colorado, Boulder Colo., 2000), p. 234.

[15] Interview with Carl Dismant Jr., May 30, 2005.

CHAPTER 3

[1] Emmons, S.F. and Hayes, C.W., *Contributions to Economic Geology* (Government Printing Office, Washington D.C., 1905), p. 62.

[2] Burbank, W.S., *U.S. Dept. of the Interior Geological Survey Bulletin 906-E: Structural Control of Ore Deposition in the Uncompahgre District, Ouray County, Colorado* (United States Government Printing Office, Washington D.C., 1940), p. 213.

[3] Rickard, T.A., *Across the San Juan Mountains* (Bear Creek Publishing Co., Ouray, Colorado, 1907), p. 9.

[4] Emmons, S.F. and Hayes, C.W., op cit, p. 60.

[5] Rickard, T.A., op. cit., p. 10.

[6] Burbank, W.S., op. cit., p. 227.

[7] Burbank, W.S., op. cit., p. 228.

[8] Plat of the Bachelor Royal, Bachelor, Aberdeen, Old Admonition and Dick Bland Lodes, Mineral Survey No. 9614, Uncompahgre Mining Dist., records of the County of Ouray, Colorado. [9] Emmons, S.F. and Hayes, C.W., op. cit., p. 60.

[10] Mining Deed Book 62, records of the Ouray County Clerk & Recorder, p. 96.

[11] Emmons & Hayes, op. cit., p. 62.

[12] *Ouray County Herald*, March 8, 1940.

[13] *Ouray County Herald & Plaindealer*, May 3, 1935.

[14] Emmons & Hayes, op. cit., p. 62.

[15] Ibid.

[16] Interview with Carl Dismant Jr., May 30, 2005.

[17] Interview with Carl Dismant Jr., May 30, 2005.

[18]   Wallace, Robert, *The Old West: The Miners* (Time-Life Books, Inc., Alexandria VA, 1976), p. 76.

[19] Smith, Duane A., *Song of the Hammer and Drill* (University Press of Colorado, Boulder Colo., 2000), p. 141.

[20] *Ouray Herald & Plaindealer*, January 30, 925.

[21] *Ouray Herald & Plaindealer*, June 30, 1925.

[22] *Ouray Herald & Plaindealer*, July 31, 1925.

[23] Interview with Carl Dismant, May 30, 2005.

[24] *Ouray Herald & Plaindealer*, May 6, 1927.

[25] Interview with Carl Dismant Jr., May 30, 2005.

[26] Rice, Frank, *The Mines of Ouray County* (Bear Creek Publishing Co., Ouray, Colorado, 1980), p. 4.

[27] Interview with Dick Zanett, May 3, 2005.

[28] Interview with Carl Dismant Jr., May 30, 2005.

[29] Interview with Al Fedel, March 3, 1998.

[30] Bachman, David, and Bacigalupi, Tod, *The Way It Was* (Wayfinder Press, Ouray Colo., 1990), p. 107.

[31] Kloepfer, Lee, *I Remember Ouray, Colorado* (Copy Setters, Lakewood Colo., 1984), p. 53.

[32] Interview with Carl Dismant Jr., May 30, 2005.

CHAPTER 4

[1] *Ouray County Herald*, March 27, 1942.

[2] Lode Record 11, records of the County of Ouray, Colorado, p. 244

[3] Smith, Duane A., *Song of the Hammer and Drill* (University Press of Colorado, Boulder Colo., 2000), p. 108.

[4] Wallace, Robert, *The Old West: The Miners* (Time-Life Books, Inc., Alexandria VA, 1976), p. 33

[5] Wallace, op. cit., p. 104.

[6] Bolognani, Bonifacio, *A Courageous People from the Dolomites* (Typilithography T.E.M.I., Trento, Italy, 1996), p. 57

[7] Interview with Gemma Mattivi, June 28, 2005.

[8] Smith, op. cit., p. 146

[9] Bolognani, op. cit., p. 200.

[10] Interview with Gemma Mattivi, June 28, 2005.

[11] Interview with Gerald Swanson, June 11, 2005.

[12] Interview with Gemma Mattivi, June 28, 2005.

[13] Smith, op. cit., p. 140.

[14] Smith, op. cit., p. 186.

[15] Smith, op. cit., p. 181.

[16] Conlin, Joseph R, *Bacon, Beans, and Galantines* (University of Nevada Press, Reno NV, 1986), p. 129.

[17] Conlin, op.cit., p. 129.

[18] Swanson, Gerald, *Swanee's Silverton* (Western Reflections Publishing Colo., Montrose Colo., 2003), p. 14

[19] Conlin, op. cit., p. 134.

[20] Ibid.

[21] Interview with Al Fedel, March 3, 1998.

[22] Interview with Elwood Gregory, June 19, 2005.

[23] Interview with Jack Clark, June 11, 2005.

[24] Wallace, op. cit., p. 24.

[25] King, Alfred Castner, *The Passing of the Storm* (Fleming H. Revell Co., New York, 1907), p. 9-10.

[26] King, Alfred Castner, *The Spirit of Freedom is Born of the Mountains, Mountain Idylls and Other Poems* (Fleming H. Revell Co., New York, 1901), p. 33.

CHAPTER 5

[1] Interview with Al Fedel, March 3, 1998.

[2] Friggens, Myriam, *Tales, Trails and Tommyknockers* (Johnson Publishing Co., Boulder Colo. 1979), p. 93.

[3] America Zoo website, <http://www.americazoo.com>.

[4] Interview with John Crim, Jan. 27, 1998.

[5] *Ouray Herald*, August 15, 1895.

[6] Interview with Louis Duke, June 18, 2005.

[7] Interview with Carl Dismant Jr., May 30, 2005.

[8] Interview with Al Fedel, March 3, 1998.

References
Photographs and Illustrations

p. i.i. Reference cover photo. The men of the Bachelor Mine (cover photo) pose with their dogs at the mine, circa 1890. Source: Rosenstock '56. *Denver Public Library, Western History Collection, X-61106*

p. i.i. Reference back cover: 1886 map of the Red Mountain Mining Region, Source: Ouray County Attorney's office, *San Juan County Historical Society;* Miners inside a mine building in Ouray County, Colorado, *Denver Public Library, Western History Collection, X-61113;* Louis Duke, blacksmith, Bachelor/Syracuse Mine Tour, *Craig Henry.*

p. i.v. Plat of the Claim of George R. Hurlburt et. al. Known as the Bachelor Royal, Bachelor Aberdeen, Old Admonition and Dick Bland Lodes.

Chapter 1

p. 2 The Diggers performing at the Bachelor/Syracuse outdoor cafe, 1995. © *Mary McCready*

p. 3 George Hurlburt as a young man, circa 1892. *Ouray County Historical Society Collection*

p. 4 Chief Ouray and his wife, Chipeta. *Ute Indian Museum, Montrose*

p. 5 Hurlburt & Wheeler Surveyors ad that appeared in the *Solid Muldoon* throughout the last half of the 1880s and into the 1890s.

p. 6 Miners pose near the shafthouse of the avalanche-prone Virginius Mine on Mount Sneffels, circa 1910. Charley Armstrong was buried by an avalanche at the Virginius. *Denver Public Library, Western History Collection, X-62115*

p. 7 A miner leads a mule train down an icy, snow-covered trail toward a mill in Ouray County, Colorado. *Denver Public Library, Western History Collection, Walker Art Studio, X-61994*

p. 8 Jesse Frank Sanders. *Delta Historical Museum*

p. 9 Only four mines appear on Red Canyon Creek (Dexter Creek) in this 1886 map of the Red Mountain Mining Region. Source: Ouray County Attorney's office. *San Juan County Historical Society*

p. 10 The miner on the right holds a singlejack hammer, which can be wielded with one hand while holding the steel drill with the other hand. Source: Rosenstock '56. *Denver Public Library, Western History Collection, X-61105*

p. 11 Three miners in the Pony Express Mine, later a part of the Bachelor Group. Working by candlelight, two of the men use a hand steel and a doublejack to drive a blasting hole. One man hits the steel with the large doublejack hammer while the other turns the steel a quarter turn after each blow. The fellow on the ladder holds a pick. Circa 1890. *Denver Public Library, Western History Collection, X-61081*

p. 12 Cora Hickman Hurlburt, circa 1895. *Ouray County Historical Society Collection*

p. 13 George Hurlburt, circa 1924, about the time he ran for Ouray County Surveyor. *Courtesy Cora Kay (Hurlburt) McCarty*

p. 14 Tombstone of George Hurlburt, Cedar Hill Cemetery, Ouray, Colorado. © *Louis Duke*

p. 15 Mail order catalog ad, circa 1890.

p. 16 Tom Walsh. *Ouray County Historical Society Collection*

p. 17 Charles Armstrong's tombstone, Cedar Hill Cemetery, Ouray, Colorado. © *Jane Bennett*

p. 18 The J. Frank Sanders home in Delta, Colorado, circa 1900. The home was torn down in June of 1986 to make way for a parking lot. *Delta Historical Museum*

CHAPTER 2
p. 19 Gold Hill. © *Louis Duke*

p. 20 Photo of Blowout today, taken from across the Uncompahgre River looking east. © *Louis Duke*

p. 21 Section along the east side of Uncompahgre Canyon through the Ouray Stock ("The Blowout"), Figure 7, Page 10. Taken from *Mines, Mountain Roads and Rocks,* by George Moore, Guidebook No. 1, Ouray County Historical Society Guidebook Series, Ouray, Colorado 2004. Adapted from Burbank, W.S., 1930, Revision of geologic structure and stratigraphy in the Ouray District of Colorado, and its bearing on ore deposition: Colorado Scientific Society Proceedings, vol. 12, no. 6., p. 151-232.

p. 23 Left: Along the Gold Belt Trail. A miner and two burros loaded with supplies, circa 1885. Collection, W. H. Jackson sample album; Colorado Book III; no. 66. *Denver Public Library, Western History Collection, William Henry Jackson, 1843-1942,* WHJ-561

p. 24 Windham Silver Mining and Smelting Company operations near Ouray, Colorado. A mule train makes its way down the hill (on the right), circa 1885. Source: Samuel Tanenbaum. *Denver Public Library, Western History Collection, X-60848*

p. 25 Frame lodging house at Windham (see photo on left; house is on right of picture). Notice the birdcage by the door, small child in front by the baby carriage and woman riding sidesaddle on the far left. Circa 1885. Source: Samuel Tanenbaum. *Denver Public Library, Western History Collection, X-14165*

p. 26 Miners near Ouray. Notice boy on the left and the fellow with the snappy straw "boater" and pipe on the right. Circa 1885. Source: Rosenstock '56. *Denver Public Library, Western History Collection, X-61105*

p. 27 Miners pose at the Calliope Silver Mine, Ouray, Colorado, 1884. Source: Rosenstock '56. *Denver Public Library, Western History Collection, G.H.A. Photo, X-61102*

p. 28 Illustration of Bachelor Dike by T.A. Rickard in *Across the San Juan Mountains*, 1907.

p. 29 Clastic dike as seen from U.S. Highway 550 at mile marker 101. © *Louis Duke*

p. 30 Sketch map of the geology and mines of the Ouray area, Figure 4, Page 5. Taken from *Mines, Mountain Roads and Rocks*, by George Moore, Guidebook No. 1, Ouray County Society Guidebook Series, Ouray, Colorado 2004. Adapted from Kelley, V.C., 1957c, Geology of Ouray and Environs, *in* Guidebook of Southwestern San Juan Mountains Colorado, New Mexico Geological Society 8th Field Conference, p. 203-207. Numbered mine names and locations from Kelley 1957c. Unencumbered mine names and locations from Luedke R.G. and W.S. Burbank, 1981, Geologic Map of the Uncompahgre (Ouray) Mining District, South Western Colorado, U.S. Geological Survey Misc. Invest. Series Map I-1247.

p. 31 Ash, circa 1900. Khedive Portal is on the lower left connected to the mill (center of photo) by rail. Boardinghouse may be on the right. Houses are scattered up the hillside. Notice the piles of lumber in the foreground to be used at the mine. *Ouray County Historical Society Collection*

p. 32 Three horse teams (yes — count 'em) at Ash loaded with supplies for the mines, circa 1900. *Ouray County Historical Society Collection*

p. 33 Miner's wife and children in front of a board and batten cabin, Ouray County, Colorado. Two of the children are boys and ride a mule, the little girl and the mother stand on the porch holding hands. Source: Frank Pecchio, Ouray. *Denver Public Library, Western History Collection, X-61353*

p. 34 A little boy and girl fishing at Lake Lenore, circa 1900. *Ouray County Historical Society Collection*

p. 35 Miners pose with shovels between a Rio Grande Southern (RGS) boxcar and a mine building in Ouray County, Colorado (possibly Bachelor Switch). Circa, 1885. Source: Frank Pecchio, Ouray. *Denver Public Library, Western History Collection, X-61112*

p. 36 Miners pose outdoors in their best clothes at a mine in Ouray County, Colorado. Snow covers the ground. Are they on their way to Lake Lenore? Circa 1890. Source: Grant U. Marcy, Ouray. *Denver Public Library, Western History Collection, X-61109*

p. 37 Skating party, Lake Lenore, circa 1890. Could the white, two-story building in the background be the "Sporting House?" Notice the lack of trees; timber had been cut for the mines. *Ouray County Historical Society Collection*

p. 38 Wettengel tombstone, Cedar Hill Cemetery, Ouray, Colorado. *© Louis Duke*

Chapter 3

p. 39 Geological section of Gold Hill. *Geologic Atlas of the United States. Ouray Folio. Colorado. No. 153. U.S. Geological Survey Washington DC 1907. S.J. Kubel, Chief Engraver. Used under public domain fair use policy*

p. 40 Type of silver-bearing vein, modified by replacement and bedding fault. *Illustration by T.A. Rickard in Across the San Juan Mountains, 1907*

p. 41 Section of American Nettie ore bodies. *After J.D. Irving, U.S. Geological Survey. From T.A. Rickard in Across the San Juan Mountains, 1907*

p. 43 Left: View west on Eighth (8th) Avenue, Ouray, Colorado, of a street crowded with teams of horses and mules hitched to wagons loaded for the mines. The Denver & Rio Grande Railroad depot and train depot and trains show across the Uncompahgre River in distance. 1892. Source: Ross Beaber. *Denver Public Library, Western History Collection, X-12822*

p. 43 An ore wagon loaded with high-grade ore and pulled by a six horse team ready to head down to town. Behind it, miners' houses and a shop building with barrels on the dock. Source: Walker Art Studios Montrose, Colo. *Denver Public Library, Western History Collection, X-62041*

p. 44 Ash in the winter. Building in the center is probably the Bachelor Boardinghouse. *Ouray County Historical Society Collection*

p. 45 Two miners working by candlelight tend a diamond drill rig one mile underground in a mine near Ouray Colorado. Circa 1885. *Denver Public Library, Western History Collection, X-61079*

p. 46 A miner poses with his cat near a mine operation in Ouray County, Colorado. Another miner poses near the shafthouse. *Denver Public Library, Western History Collection, X-61975*

p. 49 The men of the Bachelor Mine (cover photo) pose with their dogs at the mine, circa 1890. Source: Rosenstock '56. *Denver Public Library, Western History Collection, X-61106*

p. 51 Left: Miners inside a mine building in Ouray County, Colorado. Pieces of ore litter the floor. Circa 1895. Source: Frank Pecchio, Ouray. *Denver Public Library, Western History Collection, X-61113*

p. 53 Above: The Ash complex in 1900. *Ouray County Historical Society Collection*

Below: The same view as it appears today. The tailings pile in the center of the picture above is to the left in the photograph below. It's interesting to note how much the area has returned to its former state with little reclamation effort... of course, Dexter Creek helped. *© Louis Duke*

p. 54 In the early 1900s, Charley Armstrong bought his partners out and built a mill near the

Bachelor Mine to treat lower-grade ore. *Ouray County Historical Society Collection*

p. 55 Remains of the Bachelor Mill at Ash as they appear today. Note that Dexter Creek took out the two lower levels of the mill. All that's left is the topmost level. © *Louis Duke*

p. 57 Men and women pose by the abandoned American Nettie mill near Ouray, Colorado. Automobiles are parked nearby. Between 1910 and 1920. The complex is visible from U.S. Highway 550 on the west side of the Uncompahgre River. *Denver Public Library, Western History Collection, X-61998*

Chapter 4

p. 61 San Juan miner in his cabin. Notice the "homey touches" of flowers, photos, tablecloth and books. "Pinups" and scenic photographs decorate the walls above his table. Circa 1890. *Denver Public Library, Western History Collection, X-61351*

p. 62 View of a placer mining operation, shows nozzles spraying water on a river bank, near Dallas, Ouray County, Colorado. This is the Dallas Creek Day Use Area of Ridgway State Park today. *Denver Public Library, Western History Collection, WHJ-663*

p. 63 St. John's Episcopal Church in Ouray is over 100 years old and was built mostly by and for the Cornish miners. © *James Burke*

p. 65 Miners pose on a mountain in Ouray County, Colorado. One man aims a rifle. Circa 1920. Source: Frank Pecchio, Ouray. *Denver Public Library, Western History Collection, X-61119*

p. 67 Miners at a mine in Ouray County, Colorado. The men hold various tools that include planes, mallets, and saws. Circa 1885. Source: Rosenstock '56. *Denver Public Library, Western History Collection, X-61105*

p. 68 Miners pose outdoors a mine in Ouray County, Colorado. Snow covers the ground, circa 1885. Source: Grant U Marcy- Ouray. *Denver Public Library, Western History Collection, X-61111*

p. 69 Miners pose for a group portrait at a Ouray County mine. Notice cook in white apron on left. Circa 1895. Source: Henry W. Rathmell. *Denver Public Library, Western History Collection, N. H. Conley, X-62070*

p. 71 Ad for fine whiskey and champagne that appeared throughout the 1880s in *Solid Muldoon*, Ouray, Colorado.

p. 72 Western Hotel, Ouray Colorado, today. © *James Burke*

p. 72 Cook at the Bachelor Mine *Denver Public Library, Western History Collection, X-61106*

p. 73 Dining hall inside a mine's boardinghouse, Ouray County, Colorado. Notice how formally the tables are set with china dinnerware. Circa 1900. Source: Mabel Barbee Lee Photo Album 210 (C). *Denver Public Library, Western History Collection, Mabel Barbee, X-62051*

p. 75 Left: Man working at an outdoor blacksmith shop. Shows an anvil, a bellows and a forge, pickaxes, hammers, and a woodpile. Notice the *Ouray Herald* newspaper on the ground. August 10, 1897. Collection Thomas M. McKee Collection. Source Source: T.J. McKee. *Denver Public Library, Western History Collection,* Thomas Michael McKee, *Z-1262*

p. 76 Miners sharpen drills with a sledge hammer and anvil in a mine shop, Ouray County, Colorado. Interior walls are hung with hoses and tools. Circa 1900. Source: Grant U. Marcy - Ouray. *Denver Public Library, Western History Collection, X-62023*

p. 77 Lathes and drill presses fill the interior of a machine shop at a Ouray County mine, circa 1910. Source: Astoria Books. *Denver Public Library, Western History Collection, X-62024*

p. 78 Alfred Castner King, poet, was blinded by a premature explosion at the Bachelor Mine, *From* Mountain Idylls and Other Poems *by Alfred Castner King, Fleming H. Revell Company, NY and London 1901*

p. 80 Sneffels Range. © *Roger Young*

CHAPTER 5

p. 81 Lake Lenore, circa 1900. Jackass Flats is the rocky ledge above the lake. *Ouray County Historical Society Collection*

p. 82 Pack train led by a man in overalls on a horse; shows mules loaded with supplies and timbers headed for Gold Hill. Note the "Fox's Ear" peak in the background (top), a landmark on the "Amphitheater" near Ouray. Circa 1910. Collection L. C. McClure collection, 1890-1935; album III. *Denver Public Library, Western History Collection, Louis Charles McClure, G.H.A. Photo, MCC-3262*

p. 83 Patient and hardy, the burro held a special place in the hearts of miners. *Ouray County Historical Society Collection.*

p. 84 White-throated wood rat, can get as big as 14 inches, although half of that is tail! ©*Paul Berquiest*

p. 85 The ring-tailed cat, also called the "miner's pet.' ©*Paul Berquiest.*

p. 85 Little brown bat. These little guys like to hibernate for short periods of time. They like mines because the temperature remains about stable in all seasons. ©*Merlin D. Tuttle, Bat Conservation International.*

p. 87 Mysterious "Tommyknocker" visits the Bachelor/Syracuse...

p. 88 Marmot. © *Roger Young*

p. 89 Marmot outside a mine in the San Juans. When the men and the mines are gone, the marmots will probably still be here. © *Brian Jacobs*

Bibliography

Abstract of Testimony, John A. Thompson v. Thomas F. Walsh. (Douglas Taylor & Co., Law Printers, New York, 1905), 21.

America Zoo, <http://www.americazoo.com>.

Bachman, David, and Bacigalupi, Tod. *The Way it Was* (Wayfinder Press, Ouray Colo., 1990), 107.

Bolognani, Bonifacio. *A Courageous People from the Dolomites* (Typilithography T.E.M.I., Trento, Italy, 1996), 57, 200.

Bowen, A.W. *Progressive Men of Western Colorado* (A.W. Bowen & Co., Chicago IL, 1905), 360.

Burbank, W.S. *U.S. Dept. of the Interior Geological Survey Bulletin 906-E: Structural Control of Ore Deposition in the Uncompahgre District, Ouray County, Colorado* (United States Government Printing Office, Washington D.C., 1940), 191, 213, 227, 228.

Clark, Jack, Interview, June 11, 2005.

Colorado Mining Assn. 1952 Year Book, 127.

Conlin, Joseph R. *Bacon, Beans, and Galantines* (University of Nevada Press, Reno NV, 1986), 129, 134.

Crim, John, Interview, January 27, 1998.

Delta County Independent, August 7, 1895.

Dismant, Carl Jr., Interview, May 30, 2005.

Duke, Louis, Interview, June 18, 2005.

Emmons, S.F. and Hayes, C.W. *Contributions to Economic Geology* (Government Printing Office, Washington D.C., 1905), 62.

Fedel, Al, Interview, March 3, 1998.

Friggens, Myriam. *Tales, Trails and Tommyknockers* (Johnson Publishing Co., Boulder Colo. 1979), 93.

Gregory, Doris, *History of Ouray* (Cascade Publications, Ouray Colo., 1995), 279.

---. ed. *Ouray County Cemeteries* (Cedar Hill Cemetery District, Ouray Colo., 1986), 6.

Gregory, Elwood, Interview, June 19, 2005.

Hall, Frank. *History of the State of Colorado, Volume 4* (Blakely Printing Co., Chicago IL, 1889-1895, 4 Volumes), 251.

Henn, Roger. *Lies, Lore and Legends of the San Juans* (Western Reflections Publishing Co., Montrose Colo., 1999), 113.

King, Alfred Castner. *The Passing of the Storm* (Fleming H. Revell Co., New York, 1907), 9-10.

---. *The Spirit of Freedom is Born of the Mountains, Mountain Idylls and Other Poems* (Fleming H. Revell Co., New York, 1901), 33.

Kloepfer, Lee. *I Remember Ouray, Colorado* (Copy Setters, Lakewood Colo., 1984), 53.

Koch, David R., Curator. *George Hurlburt, The Life & Times of a San Juan Surveyor*, Ouray County Historical Society (Ouray Colo.; 1984), 1, 5.

Kushner, Ervan F. *A Guide to Mineral Collecting at Ouray Colorado* (Ervan F. Kushner Books, Paterson, New Jersey, 1973), 3, 7, 50, 64.

Lode Record 11. Records of the County of Ouray, Colorado, 244.

Mattivi, Gemma, Interview, June 28, 2005.

Mining Deed Book 38. Records of the Ouray County Clerk & Recorder, 161.

Mining Deed Book 62. Records of the Ouray County Clerk & Recorder, 96.

Ouray Herald, August 15, 1895.

Ouray County Herald, December 29, 1939.

---, March 8, 1940.

---, March 27, 1942.

Ouray Herald & Plaindealer, Feb. 17, 1921.

---, October 26, 1924.

---, June 30, 1925.

---, July 31, 1925.

---, May 6, 1927.

---, May 3, 1935.

Ouray Times, August 11, 1877.

Plat of the Bachelor Royal, Bachelor, Aberdeen, Old Admonition and Dick Bland Lodes, Mineral Survey No. 9614, Uncompahgre Mining Dist., records of the County of Ouray, Colorado.[9] Emmons, S.F. and Hayes, C.W., 60.

Rathmell, Ruth. *Of Record and Reminiscence* (North Suburban Printing & Publishing, Inc., Westminister Colo., 1976), 56.

Rathmell, Judge William. Unpublished manuscript, "History of Ouray County," 1940, 22.

Rice, Frank. *The Mines of Ouray County* (Bear Creek Publishing Co., Ouray, Colorado, 1980), 4.

Rice, Frank. Unpublished manuscript, "History of Ouray County and Its Mines," Ouray, Colorado, 1961.

Rickard, T.A. *Across the San Juan Mountains* (Bear Creek Publishing Co., Ouray, Colorado, 1907), 9, 10.

Smith, Duane A. *Song of the Hammer and Drill* (University Press of Colorado, Boulder Colo., 2000), 108, 140, 141, 146, 181, 186, 234.

The Solid Muldoon, June 22, 1883.

---, Feb. 29, 1884.

Swanson, Gerald, Interview, June 11, 2005.

Swanson, Gerald. *Swanee's Silverton* (Western Reflections Publishing Colo., Montrose Colo., 2003), 14.

Wallace, Robert. *The Old West: The Miners* (Time-Life Books, Inc., Alexandria VA, 1976), 24, 33, 76, 104, 178.

Zanett, Dick, Interview, May 3, 2005.

Index